To Don

Finally Freed

" Be a warrior who overcomes unlisted boundaries!"

TJ KECHULA

ISBN 978-1-64258-650-3 (paperback)
ISBN 978-1-64258-651-0 (digital)

Christian Faith Publishing, Inc.
832 Park Avenue
Meadville, PA 16335
www.christianfaithpublishing.com

I have recreated events, locales and conversations from my memories of them. In order to maintain their anonymity in most instances I have changed the names of individuals and places, I may have changed some identifying characteristics and details such as physical properties, occupations and places of residence.

Printed in the United States of America

NOTE FROM THE AUTHOR

I began this journey October 23rd, 2013.

This was a road I never again cared to journey down.
To the center of my trauma.
However, because of it I am a changed woman.

-T J Kechula

ACKNOWLEDGEMENTS

First and foremost, I want to acknowledge God. Without Him, the story in this book would never have been possible to revisit, much less write. I thank you God for healing me from the inside out. This journey has only just begun. You are so amazingly beautiful! I owe my life to You, Lord.

I want to give a special thanks to my husband, Mark and my son, Tyler for always being there to lend me support, to cheer me on, to keep me going, and to never let me give up. I dedicate this book to you guys, my most favorite people in this world, for being my friends and my family. Thank you both dearly. I love you SO much!

Rest in peace Dad. To my loving mother: "You did not know the secrets, as they were mine to bear. The threats were far too difficult to challenge as a small child." I have never once placed blame on my parents. They were simple people, who lived simple lives. I love you Mom.

To all my family who get to finally know what happened to that little girl so many years ago; the one who appeared to be troubled; the one who appeared to be broken; the one who was surely misunderstood: Be gentle and kind to the unknown. You never know what someone else is going through. Especially when it's a child who's too afraid to tell.

To my Thursday night CCC bible study group: God used you to help me grow. I thank you ladies for never being judgmental, not once! You rock!

To my Hampton Roads friends: Thank you for your love and support.

To my Finally Freed Facebook Group and my Facebook community: I want to thank each of you but there's simply not enough room! Your encouragement was heartfelt and special. You were always there when I needed your support. Thank you Diane Safara DeSellems, for being an Administrator on the Finally Freed Facebook group and keeping it a peaceful, pleasant place to visit.

To my bestie cousins and friends in Florida: You have been a constant in my existence on planet earth. Life would not be the same without you. Thank you for always listening to my stories.

To my niece way down in southern Florida: You first read my journals as the disorganized works they were. You never knew how much it meant to me when your tears fell. I knew at that moment that it was okay to share my story with the world. Thank you for your kind and gentle spirit.

To my friend Ann, from Richmond, Virginia: Thank you for your prayers and support. Thank you for reading and helping me gather my journals into a more organized fashion. Every step was a process with progress!

Thank you to my sister-in-law Sharon, for helping me with the final touches in this book. I will always be grateful.

Thank you to The Kechula Family, you accepted me into your family, without ever knowing what I had just escaped from, a year before.

To my friend Vickie: You always welcomed me to the ranch with open arms. Riding horses during the writing of Finally Freed gave me more therapy than you will ever know. Thank you, to you and Terry, for being my family too.

To my friend, spiritual sister, and personal photographer: Thank you Leah Tennant. You did a wonderful job with the author photos.

Thank you to my Christian therapist, Don MacKay: May God's blessings be with you always! God used you to teach me the way to freedom. You gave me book after book as homework to read. You challenged me to work hard. I listened to God's message, and through you, I slowly began to peel, to reveal, and to heal from the folds of trauma that were so deeply embedded into my memory. I came to so many monumental moments of success in healing. There, I obtained an even higher understanding of God's plan. I learned how to give healthy self-love. I also learned that I will always be growing inside this journey of life. Don, thank you for being the compassionate clinical therapist that you are. Thank you for being there every single week for over four years.

Prior to October 2013, when I first began this journey, I had no idea who I was. I had no confidence as to where I belonged in this world. I Facebook messaged my church. "If I fell to my knees would you be there to lift me up? I am desperate, I need help." Help came in the form of the pastor's wife praying with me. *Thank you, Donna.* While she prayed, I opened my eyes to see her earnest commitment and her compassion for my brokenness. Suddenly God opened a portal to heaven. This is when I first knew what God's love really felt like. It bended my once thoughtless perception about love and spirituality. This is when that vibrant shining light entered my once dim existence. The same light that has progressively shined brighter every day that I walk in it.

Welcome to where it all began for me as a child.

CONTENTS

PROLOGUE
PUTTING IT ALL BEHIND ME

1990 (27 Years Old)

I was never so amazed as when I rode with my sister and brother-in-law through the Keys. We were heading south for Key West, to the land of the unknown. Unknown to me, anyway. I had no idea of what it would be like. All I knew was that the further southbound we went, perhaps the less restless I would feel.

En route, I began seeing the difference in landscape. I sat back in my seat, hugging the window, and as the fresh air began taking on a more coastal essence, I savored the familiar metallic taste of salt. I watched the change of landscape unfold before my eyes as the palm trees fluttered gracefully. The small towns were separated by an open view of the endless saltwater delight. Powerfully magical was the pristine translucence of aquamarine waters accented with brightly lit diamonds on their caps.

I thought, *there could never be scenery that would trump this majestic beauty.* I felt guided to this place for much needed rest, a haven of peace and tranquility. Yet, in the hollows of my chest sat that big lump that simply wouldn't move. It was wedged in as a reminder that I was in a deep state of grieving.

The day before, I had taken my sister Caroline and her husband Henry into the bathroom at our parents' house. I needed to ask them for two things, knowing I could no longer stay in my hometown.

I had to have time to regroup and heal from the trauma I had escaped from only months before.

I humbly asked them both, "Please help me."

As I began to cry, Caroline embraced me, her youngest sister. "What do you need, Tammie?"

"I can't stay here. There are too many questions. People want answers. I don't want to remember what happened. Not now. Not like this. I need to learn how to live again. How to heal. How to forgive." I said.

Henry added, "You were with Kevin for a very long time. People ask because they are curious, Tammie, about what happened to you while you were gone. Someday they will ask you why you didn't leave sooner."

I blew my nose gently, "I can't answer them. I need time to heal. I desperately need to get away, and that's why I've pulled you guys in here, so no one can hear us."

Caroline searched my tormented expression, "Sister, just come right out with it, what can we do to help you."

I needed clarity as I swallowed my pride, "I need to ask if you can take me home with you to Key West. Also, if you could give me one hundred dollars. I will get a job and my own place as soon as I save some money. I'll pay you back with my first paycheck. All I need is one chance."

They did not even hesitate. Henry reached for his wallet from his back pocket and pulled out five twenties and handed them to me. Caroline's eyes glistened with tears as she looked on at me. She knew some of what I had gone through, the struggle to free myself from the wrath of the man I had been with, as well my dire need to leave my hometown.

Caroline said, "of course we will help you, we leave tomorrow morning. Is that too soon for you to be ready?"

Feeling the world just being lifted off my shoulders, I answered with much relief, "No, it isn't too soon. I have only a few things. I will need to buy clothes after I get a job. I can't thank you both enough for helping me. I will never forget this for the rest of my life."

It was all so complicated, but I felt safe and cared for by them, at least for the moment. I knew I would never take advantage of their kindness, nor ever let them down. It was just something I was convinced of. A part of me knew that I was being led by a supreme cloud of guidance. These family members were enabling me to get my life back on track, and I never once believed it was *by chance.*

Even while the tropical scenery slid past my view, my world stood still. I was traveling in the backseat of their white Bronco. Silently, I was trying to take it all in. To digest it. I had absolutely no clue where I was going nor what lay ahead. Nor did I understand the psychology of *why* a person would grieve over a perpetrator. Or was the grieving for the death of something else? No matter how bad it had been during all those years, I'd survived! I wasn't going to be bitter over lost years either. I had never allowed myself to be snarly and bitter before. I wanted desperately to celebrate that I had lived through it!

Kevin's pernicious design had been to convince me that he had powers over me. He said that he saved me from myself and from my childhood trauma. He filled me with empty dreams and crushed my spirit.

It seemed so long ago, as I sat numb in my memories. I knew nothing about the world around me, and most certainly didn't want anyone to know how naïve I really was. I didn't want sympathy from people, and most definitely not their pity! I wanted to be treated as an equal. I never wanted to fail, especially since he had spent the past 12 years of my life convincing me that I would.

In my hometown, I had been around my family and friends and their questions about what happened, why had I never told anyone, and what was I going to do with my life now. I couldn't keep facing them all at that moment. I sat thinking of how far I had come just to get to that distant place called The Southernmost Point.

In searching my heart, I knew I had reached my new home. It was also the furthest distance I could go without leaving the country. *Which,* I mused, *wouldn't be a bad idea either.*

My exposure to America was halted when Kevin moved me out into that barren desert 12 years before. I didn't really know what to expect from my future. I was being exposed to so many elements of change. I reflected, *how am I to live in the civilized world and not stick out? I lived that life of seclusion for so long!*

In the end, God had showed up in the wilderness. He came to that desert on that final night, with His plan. He showed His power over Kevin, as Kevin laid still on that floor. God took over as He said, *it is finished, it is enough*. From that night on, where He lead, I followed.

Now, because of God's glory, I will finally be able to live the rest of my life in freedom!

This is my journey.

I vow to never take advantage of this life called my own.

CHAPTER ONE

The Place Called Home

1973 (11 Years Old)

I was born Tammie Jean. Momma always told me that it was the delivery nurse who named me.

I grew up in a small rural town in north Florida, but I always knew that one day I would leave that place I called home. The cost was greater to stay under the threats of my abusers, than to break away and leave forever. My childhood roots grew deep and jagged. From an early age, I was sexually assaulted by distant relatives. I'd felt I had failed terribly by never revealing those secrets to my parents. The challenges of growing up in a jungle of unknown enemies, left the quiet little girl inside me confused as to what love was.

My parents loved each other and had five babies to prove it. We were spread out over more than a twenty-year span with Ben being the last of us and born when I was 10 years old. My parents had been divorced and remarried several times, to each other. Yet theirs was a true symbol of dedication and never giving up. They raised their family as best they could with love and grace. We all went to church every Sunday and learned about God and worship. We were always playing ball, riding horses, or working together harvesting vegetables from the garden in the back yard.

As a little girl, I recall standing on the back porch on Sunday mornings, getting ready for church. There would be me, Caroline, Victor, and Bridgette, all brushing our teeth outside. We would spit down into the white sand gully, which was formed from the downpour of rain where it ran off the roof. There would be no television on, no radios blaring; just the sounds of birds and nature. I was the baby of the family and I loved that special time with my older siblings. I admired each of them in their own ways. I felt safe and protected when I was at home with my family.

My daddy worked long, hard hours painting houses. I remember how tired he'd be when he got home. I would be standing at the door the minute he drove up, waiting until he came inside when he would whisk me up into his arms. My heart swelled with love for my daddy.

Then he would put me down and go straight to the shower. Patiently, I waited outside his bedroom for him to finish. When he came out he always had on a white t-shirt, a cotton button up shirt, and a pair of dress shorts. I remember how the tan-line on his legs terminated where his black dress socks stopped half way up his calves from wearing them outside in the sunshine at home. He wore his black oxford dress shoes walking around in the yard. It was just who he was.

Daddy always took a twenty-minute nap on the tan vinyl couch in the living room. I wouldn't leave his side. I watched "Leave It to Beaver" on the black and white television set, while sitting on the floor with my back against the couch, and my baby-doll, Kathy, in my arms.

My daddy's spirit was that of a gracefully quiet soul. He could fill me up with love just by calling me "Pumpkin".

Momma loved taking care of her family. She always had dinner on time, and we all had our assigned seats. Daddy didn't like a lot of noise at the table. We weren't allowed to scrape our forks on the plate, nor eat with our mouths open. Daddy said that it sounded like a bunch of pigs slopping up their food in the pen. I know he meant well by trying to teach us his values and manners.

Momma kept the house on a tight schedule; everyone had their areas to keep up. In the summertime, she gave us the chance to choose which chores we wanted to claim as ours. I didn't mind at all because I knew it pleased her when I helped. I was so young back then. Life was so much simpler.

Momma was always busy doing things to keep the house going, while Daddy worked his job. Momma didn't mind when I hung out with her. I recall wondering how one pair of hands could do so much. I loved seeing her hands roll out dough after sprinkling flour onto the tabletop. I also spent many hours next to her while she fed material through her sewing machine, making new dresses for my sisters and me.

Momma worked long hours washing and hanging clothes to dry. Then she ironed almost everything. Out in the back yard sat an electric wringer washer on a platform made of boards that kept it off the damp ground. There were many times when I stood on a coffee can next to Momma and that old washer. I watched as she meticulously fed wet items through the rotating wringer rollers. Each of the two rollers spun inwardly toward the other, grabbing the cloth that it was fed. The wringers squeezed out the excess water in the fabric that was then hung out to dry in the shine of the Florida sun. It was a fascinating process to a little kid.

One day, when I was four, Momma was inside the house cleaning with Bridgette and Caroline and I decided to take a closer look at the machine. The wringer washer was swishing and washing a load of clothes, so I grabbed my old coffee can and stepped up for a better view. I stuck my hand in the washer-basket while it was in motion, and retrieved one of my socks.

Momma had always made it look so easy. I thought I would help her out that day! Just as she did it, I courageously fed the sock through the rotating wringers. In an instant, it snatched the sock. I suppose I had a tight grip on the sock, for my hand was instantly fed in between the rollers!

Now, wringers are designed with give, for thicker materials like quilts and rugs. One must pull the lever for the rollers to disengage anything stuck between them. Yet, in the drama of it all, to a 4-year-old, it became a raging, child-eating machine! It didn't take long for those wringer rollers to ride right up my little arm as they kept on rotating inward, trying to suck the rest of me through! I was beyond terrified! My arm was on fire from the friction of the twirling rollers that wouldn't stop turning!

My screams began the second I was propelled forward. It all happened so fast! Soon enough Momma came running outside, with trembling hands she turned off the power and flipped the release lever.

"Oh, my goodness, Tammie, what have you done?" Momma cried out with tears streaming down her face.

In the aftermath of it all, I'm thinking that it looked worse than it actually was.

She whisked me up from the platform into her arms, and ran with me to our beige station wagon.

"Bridgette, get my purse and the car keys! Hurry!" She called out toward the house.

Dr. Rebel was our family doctor and knew my momma very well. He delivered many of her babies. His office was located about 15 minutes from our house in the downtown area, a few blocks from the river. As it turned out, Dr. Rebel placed a sling on my arm and gave instructions for aspirin to be given for any discomfort. He made certain to inform me to leave the clothes washing to the adults. Frankly, I was good with that.

The family moved often, to follow Daddy's jobs, but mostly to follow Grandpa and Grandma to other states, as momma loved living near her parents. For those reasons, I was never in one school for very long. But it seems we always ended up back at our roots, in the northeast corner of Florida, where the azaleas bloomed bigger and brighter than anywhere.

I have wonderful memories of growing up around family, that is, family who did not prey upon children. Those loving relatives were enjoyable to be around. In the evening time on the weekends, they would all sit around a campfire and play guitars and sing. It was always either at one of their houses or a place they called "in the woods," where we all went camping.

I can close my eyes and see my daddy playing his guitar while singing. He played with a seriousness on his face, with one eye more opened than the other. I was amazed at his ability to transform into the character of a musician. It always looked like a pirate to me. One bushy eyebrow raised high and the other lowered, he would sing out of the side of his mouth. I could recognize by the look in his eyes, that he had left his physical body and was playing inside the passion of his music, where the storyline became about him. I could feel his unconstrained passion and deep sense of loss or belonging or elation, whatever the storyline read of the song he was singing.

"Your cheating heart will make you weep,
you'll cry and cry and try to sleep.
But sleep won't come the whole night through.
Your cheating heart will tell on you."

In between songs, the aunts and uncles were always laughing and telling jokes. I loved my aunts. They were always so jovial and seemed happy enough, but I do know that a couple of them made some bad choices in the men they married and brought into our family and around us children. These men and their sons, lead secret lives of molesting little children, right behind the parents' backs.

I was as young as six when I first remember an uncle molesting me. Years went by with horribly humiliating memories of being fondled inappropriately, waking up to their hot breath on me, or the smell of them pushing their crotch on me, which stayed with me for many years.

I was tormented by the images of those men. I was covered with the shame of what they did to me; barely old enough to ride a bicycle and I was already silenced by their words. There were too many times of being silent and too many lies by not telling. They found sadistic pleasures in shattering the innocence of me and the other little girls in our family. What they'd said to me left my immature mind crushed and scarred with such undeserving pain.

I remembered being in church on any given Sunday, and listening to the sermon being preached with passion against evil doers. I just knew that I could be struck by lightning most any time. No matter the frills and lace my momma dressed me in to make me pretty, I could never be. I was ugly and dirty on the inside and I didn't understand how to wash that away.

I found it difficult to understand what normal was. Those infinite tears remained coated on the lining of my existence.

I recall the final night of visiting one of my aunt and uncles' houses. I hadn't been there for a couple of years, because we had been busy moving around to different states. He was my earliest memory of being abused, back three years earlier, when I was six. I had never stayed the night there before, but I really missed my cousin, Elizabeth. She was a year older than me.

Late in the night Uncle Fred came into the room where I was. While we were asleep, he approached the bed. My back was to the door. I immediately felt his presence and woke up, just as he laid his hand on my side. I thought maybe if I didn't move he would go away, but he remained, and his hand began to slide down.

Immediately I repelled it off me, speaking up and begging his daughter to "please make him leave me alone!"

My cousin commanded her daddy to "leave now." He did as she told him, and left the room.

It was all too unthinkable to repeat to anyone. My cousin's commanding voice to her father seemed far too mature and beyond her years. Earlier that same evening we had been on the floor playing with Barbie dolls. We were just little girls! I had never heard my cousin speak with such authority. First, she turned to me and said that she was sorry for what her father had done to me all those years. She then spoke of her own pain. She began confessing her own family's secret to me, and the darkness she lived in all her life, inside her own secret prison of abuse.

Elizabeth spoke of being afraid of her daddy. She said that he would hover over her and demand that she *do* things to him. Uncle Fred told his daughter that it was her job to have sex with him since her mother was not willing to do it. She was so scared that she had never reported this to anyone. Shame kept her from confessing to her mother. Those were the words from my ten-year-old cousin, Elizabeth.

I remember being stunned and feeling so horribly bad for my cousin. She cried this to me and I did my best to console her. I was too young to really understand the implications behind being preyed upon by adults.

I never slept over at Elizabeth's house again, or even went back there. I made excuses when my parents wanted to go. They'd always drop me off at a different relative's house, one of my own choosing. I felt bad for what was going on with Elizabeth, but I couldn't allow myself to absorb the whole picture of such deep dark secrets that were affecting the children in my family.

My parents were good to me. They didn't know of the hidden secrets behind those pedophiles who lurked around secretly hurting the little children. I believed that it would bring them shame if I confessed. The perpetrators made it quite clear to me that they would hurt my family and would say horrible things about me if I told. Then my family would throw me away and I would have to live on the streets. I lived in the terror the abusers created for me.

I slowly began disconnecting and withdrawing from my parents. I still loved them dearly. I can't explain it, but as the years progressed, my image of what normal was faded. I stopped computing love as a token of security. It became more valued, sacred, a privilege to receive. And I did not feel privileged. The filth running through my veins ran like poison.

I learned at a young age how to build walls, so no one could see me. As I grew older I blamed myself for the unmistakable ugliness that was planted so deeply inside me. That was my only rationale for

why I was chosen to be molested in the first place. All my perpetrators spoke the same language, placing the blame on my shoulders for
what *would happen* to me and my parents if I told. I was too damaged
inside to believe I was worthy of anyone understanding my story, if I
had made that decision to tell.

CHAPTER TWO

❖

Poisonous Scars

1974–1976 (12-13 Years Old)

When I turned twelve things took a turn for the worse. A new abuser surfaced among my relatives, and his evil was unmatched. He was a cousin I hadn't seen often throughout my life. At fifteen years older than me, I didn't have many memories of interacting with him. He always seemed like a nice person to me.

However, his abuse would prove to be exponentially worse than my entire childhood of abusers combined. He was a darker, more violently sinister criminal, than I could ever have imagined a human to be.

It was the weekend and all the parents were going out partying. The wives were all dolled up, with their hair teased high with half a can of hair spray. The men, with their hair combed back, shining with gel, and smelling strongly of cologne. They were all going dancing. It was just a family thing to them. Usually between four to eight of them would all meet up at a local club just on the edge of town.

Our parents would always leave an adult relative, never strangers, in charge of the kids. It was against their rules, as they liked to feel their children were safe. Normally, it was my older sister, but for some reason she was not in the picture that night. The parents gave my older male cousins the name and phone number of the place they were going, in case of an emergency.

As it stood, we were left in the care of these older cousins, who were all over the age of eighteen. There were four of us younger children, who were twelve years of age and under.

We were all fed copious amounts of alcohol. I believe that I was the first to be taken for a drive. This unconscionable act was being carried out against the very children these men were being paid to supervise!

I was put in a pickup truck and driven down a road leading away from my aunt's house. Initially, my cousin Adam told me that my parents had called and wanted him to drive me home. Then we turned off the main road and down a dark dirt road. I can remember being paralyzed by the alcohol, but not yet scared of my surroundings. I trusted my cousin, not knowing what he was about to do. I had no reason to believe that I was in any kind of danger from him. I was just floating in a state of nothingness, not really feeling anything at all.

The truck came to a sudden stop. As I sat staring forward, a plane crossed from my right side and landed in the close distance and I knew approximately where I was. We were parallel to the local air strip. The moonless night was as dark as coal and only the lights in the far distance, across the airfield, were visible.

Adam opened his door and got out of the truck. I was not aware of any time lapse when he came to my door, and opened it. Grabbing my upper arm, he yanked me out and my feet hit hard onto the ground. He immediately caught me off guard and he began touching me *all over*! In places that were private and off limits. I struggled as hysteria set in, and everything began spinning. I was nauseated as I frantically tried slapping him away. I was crying and screaming and pleading with him to "please stop!"

All I should've wanted right then were my parents, but all I really wanted was to move to a different planet. I just wanted to be gone far, far away where there was only me and no one else to ever hurt me again.

I never once in my life blamed my parents since they didn't know any better. Perhaps they were so trusting because they both came from large families where there was lots of love and everyone cared about each other. They had grown up in a place where you could actually trust your relatives. It wasn't their fault. I was convinced of it.

I felt that familiar grieving for my lost soul which resulted from my loss of control to another smelly, sadistic human man molesting me. I was sickened with a sense of his putrid environment that dragged me down to an equal level with contaminated sewage! Slowly being stripped of my dignity, I struggled to fight him off, but he trans-morphed in something purely evil that I could not comprehend. He yanked loose the button and zipper to my cotton shorts despite my resistance.

He shamed me awake from the alcohol induced state he had caused. He shoved a balled-up piece of engine oil smelling cloth deep into my mouth, preventing my pleas from being heard. He forcefully turned me around and threw me half inside the truck as my clothes fell to the ground.

It was impossible to breathe as he pressed my face even harder into the fabric of the bench seat. The pain seared through me, like rotating razor blades cutting at me deep inside. My cries had deepened into a helplessness I could not stop. I was falling into a bottomless pit. He raped me for what seemed like forever, exhaling whispers of shameful names and unspeakable things to me. I drifted away inside a foggy existence. My mind was not there anymore. I entered a revolving door between conscious and unconscious states of mind.

There, at twelve years of age, I was being violently raped. I had lost all hope that I would survive that night. Finally, after he was done with me he told me to put my clothes back on announcing to me that I was a nothingness slut, and that I had instigated the entire thing.

He said those words to my tender ears, as they lay like rock in concrete beneath my chest. Those words, they meant nothing to him! But to me, they cost me my innocence. My sanity. He gave me one last thing to lock me inside his prison forever. He told me that he would find me, and beat me and rape me again, *whenever he wanted to.*

He continued to say awful things to me, things that made no sense at that time. His words were quite convincing with his stern tone. He would make it my fault if I ever said a word to anyone, contaminating even more of my young soul. He said that he would call me horrible names to everyone in my hometown, even at my school, *if he wanted to*. As the final blow, he told me that if I ever spoke a word to anyone, he would mess my family up bad. I didn't have to ask what that meant.

I was already so scarred from other cousins and uncles, there was no reason not to believe his violent words were any less potent. He had convinced me of his potential for violence, including murder. I believed him!

Arriving back at his mother's house, he told me to make sure I was asleep before my parents came to get me. He told me one last time, not to forget that his threats were real. I trembled at his voice. I laid waiting for my parents. I was in extreme fear for mine and my family's lives. In my 12-year-old mind I knew that he was capable of killing us.

After that, I withdrew from everyone. I feared for anyone to see inside my soul, and for that reason alone I did not walk with my head held high. They'd be able to see all the bad things I'd *allowed* to happen to me for all those years. I knew that I was labeled with ugliness, otherwise why did they all choose me?

Whenever my momma would dote about how pretty I was and how I needed to smile more, I'd press the corners of my lips up, just to please her, but I was far from being happy. I continued dressing in nothing remotely girly, unless she insisted for church or a special occasion. But only for my momma. Otherwise, I dressed to cover up everything.

When she would run her hand across my back and bottom side to make sure I had on underclothes, she had no clue how much shame I harbored. I just wanted to get away, forever, and never return.

When I turned thirteen, my parents bought me a horse. Her name was Charlie. They were always trying to win over my confidence. They knew I was troubled and just didn't know how to reach me. I loved on Charlie, brushing her daily. Petting her brought me so much peace, I'd close my eyes and whiff her scent into my memory bank. In the fall, with her horse hair growing thick at the roots it gave the appearance of a grizzly bear's fur just before hibernation. That's when I especially loved riding her bareback. With that cushion, it was like sitting on a sheep's wooly back.

I would go riding through the trails next to our house and across the railroad tracks. Every day after school I couldn't wait to saddle up and go think of nothing! It was the closest thing to complete peace that I could find. The Florida trails, with their tall pine trees and smooth dirt floors covered with a blanket of dead pine needles, became forever etched into my memory.

Early spring brought warmer temperatures and I loved being under the shaded canopy of those tall pine trees, where the air seemed fresher than in the blistering sun. Those days always reminded me of a fairytale with beautiful endings.

Sometimes, right after a summer's rain, the resulting fog would lay cradled in the tree tops, serene and quietlike. From far away you could hear the winds approaching, then watch and listen as it migrated closer, swaying the long skimpy branches of the pine trees. Nature took me away to a simpler state of forgetfulness.

One day after school, I went down to those trails as usual to go for a walk in my fairytale forest of trees. But this time I went without Charlie. It was so peaceful on that day, I remember being oblivious to anything else going on in the world around me. I felt safe.

Just in the distance, I saw a guy walking toward me on the trail. An older boy, with a familiar face. I had seen him around the older 8th grade girls at the school parking lot after school was out.

"Hey, I know you!" He said. "You're always up at the school when I'm there. I always see you. I think you're really cute."

"Thanks, but I have to get home now."

He asked, "I'm Merle Bibbs, what was your name again?"

"Tammie," I revealed for whatever reason.

He declared, "I think I want to make you my girlfriend, come over here!"

Hysteria was seeping in through my blood stream as I knew something wasn't right. I began walking faster away from him. He grabbed me and threw me down onto that pine needle floor. I tried to get loose, but he overcame my strength.

I watched as those tall pine trees swayed from side to side, as the wind picked up and the whirling sounds became louder. I thought I heard a voice saying to me,

> "keep looking up,
> don't think anymore,
> listen to the whine of the wind."

When I finally looked back down to ground level, he was gone. Slowly, I got to my feet, brushing pine needles off my exposed flesh. I gathered my clothes, and put them on, without even a single teardrop in my eye. I went straight home and poured a bath.

My mother asked where I had been, but I couldn't answer for fear of crying and not being able to stop. Caroline's response was, "probably out in the woods messing around with one of those boys down the road." She never even knew the depth of the impact that her statement made. It didn't take a brainy astronaut to know what she was insinuating. I was so utterly and completely misunderstood by everyone. I tried to believe in me for all of those who I felt didn't. Being in an environment that hypothesized on such things as immorality at the tender age of 13, gave me no true sense of belonging, anywhere.

The next morning, I left. Before anyone else was awake. I had gathered a few things and began my journey by foot. I was running away. Maybe it was a trial run for my forever escape. But I felt I needed to begin my trial runs to see how to leave, before my perpetrators hurt me again, or maybe even killed my family.

When I was found that day I was ready to be found and stepped out when I saw my family looking for me. But still, I said nothing to them, though they begged me to tell them what was bothering me.

I didn't want them to get hurt, so I said nothing. I saw no purpose in exposing them to my rapist's threats. All that could be seen from the naked eye of my family was brokenness, noncompliance, a delinquent being disobedient and running away. It was my own duty to disguise the truth of my past and live a life with undefined love.

It was tough for my parents, not being able to reach me. They would tell me *no* to a request I'd make to them, but I didn't listen most of the time. I persisted, until they gave in. I ran away frequently, never really knowing where I was going. I think, during that time in my life, it was more about following someone else. Absentmindedly, I was trying to find peace. My logic was 'why not'? Perhaps happiness and peace were somewhere out there waiting to be found.

Again, I wouldn't even have known where to begin. I couldn't bear the thought of watching the shame build in their eyes as I would reveal my lifetime of horror stories for them to hear. My abusers had all told me that it would be seen as my fault, if I had told anyway. And so, I lived on inside myself, without a way of escaping from my internal prison, and without an antidote for my perpetrator's poisons that spilled into my bloodstream.

CHAPTER THREE

—◆◆—

Parental Love

1976 (14 Years Old)

M omma and Daddy always lived simple lives with minimal needs. They loved the outdoors, country music, and having a fish fry. That was the highlight of their weekends. Momma grew up with eleven brothers and sisters who lived off the land as they farmed their own crops. Momma recalls, "we all learned about family love! We grew up with enough love for everyone!" I knew my momma's parents and they were genuinely good, loving people. Daddy's parents both passed away when I was very young, but I think they were the ones who started up the church in our township many years before. There were seven siblings on Daddy's side. I hadn't spent much time around them but the time I did, I recall the abundance of love they had for me. I always felt like I shared more physical features with them than I did with my momma's side of the family.

My parents had three children, then seven years later, they had me. When I was nine years old, my momma was with child again, and eight months later, she gave birth to the most beautiful little boy I'd ever seen. "Ben" was welcomed with arms wide opened! I decided to make him my little boy!

I tried to live as my family encouraged me to. I would laugh at the adult's jokes, I would sing songs for my momma, though surely, she realized at some point that my talent didn't lie there, and I played board games with the adults. They loved to play their Parcheesi games while Grandma kept Grandpa supplied with his glasses of buttermilk and cornbread. I never quite understood that one.

One time, when I was about eleven years old, I was helping my grandpa mow his lawn when his wallet vibrated out of his back pocket, and he ran the riding lawn mower right over it! There were pieces of paper bill money flying everywhere! It was surreal, seeing the paper and slowly realizing that it was money!

He was angry at first, over that freak accident, but I could see how Grandpa took some, if only a little, humor from the situation. I helped him pick up all the pieces of hundred-dollar bills from all over the lawn. We found every single piece, and with each serial number pieced together, the bank reimbursed for every bill torn to shreds. I loved my grandpa!

Growing up, I believed that my momma secretly dreamed, if only a tiny bit, that things could've been different for her. She always came alive when she spoke to me of what she used to dream of becoming: a fashion illustrator. She spoke in detail about creating different clothing lines through sketching out graphic designs on paper, and choosing exquisite fabrics. Still, my momma was a proud woman and loved her family.

My daddy? He loved his family too. He was a good ole country boy, turned good ole country man. He enlisted in the army at the age of 18 but had already completed his term by the time he and Momma got married.

◆

In my mind, living at home with my parents only placed us all at risk for the dangers of my abuser's threats.

My image of who I was, was so distorted by my rapist's unscrupulous knack for staining my innocence. I began disassociating myself from all trauma. Completely. Every time the memories returned, I would shut them out, and myself from the world around me. It wasn't a cure, but it rather muffled out the pain that shot lasers into my reality, and into my heart.

Then nighttime would fall, and the trauma would reappear in my dreams. At times, it was so bad, so violent, that I'd completely sit up in bed and will myself to wake up and stay awake. Sometimes I'd sit like that until the light of the morning shone through the curtains. At times, from mere exhaustion, I would unintentionally dose back off just before daylight. Falling back asleep in the early morning hours was always the worst. I would fall into a deeper sleep and it became difficult for my parents to wake me for school.

That same exhaustion would creep through my veins as I would dress for school. I tried to focus on my studies in class, but always ended up laying my head down on the desk and falling asleep. Once the entire class left me there! My teacher finally woke me up. She was unkind and said something about alcohol and drugs causing sleep deprivation.

There were many times when I skipped the bus altogether. I would slip away into the woods across the road. There, past the trees was the open body of water known as the St. Johns River. The residents of the houses that lined the river, would have already left for work and I'd walk out to the end of one of their private docks and stretch out on my towel that I would already have with me in anticipation. I found peace in the warmth of the morning shine across the river. There I would go into a deep state of pure sleep. Nothing else. No nightmares, just a nourishing beautifully-woven slumber.

Being academically undisciplined was a downfall of my own. I went to school, but I don't recall learning anything. I could not tell the name of one single teacher, or even what one of them looked like.

I lived in a world of dreams where I was cleansed, happy, and far away from the horrors that sketched into my soul every time there was a family gathering. With every night that passed, after the stars had left their places in the sky, I was left dreaming still.

I really didn't understand what self-esteem was, except I knew that I had a problem. I was at an all-time low.

While I wore my semi-baggy clothes to avoid attention, a part of me wanted to blame my peers for dressing so skimpily. I deduced that they were partially to blame for creating that criminal craziness in adult men. Those girls didn't seem to understand, it wasn't only boys who were watching them. There were evil men lurking in their shadows! Those criminals who would have no respect for women and girls, regardless of the age. They would be waiting for one out of ten of them to pass that dark corner while no one else was watching.

Being raped makes you a believer in nightmares. I constantly dreamed of when I'd leave.

I loved being around my cousins that I was close to growing up, and that were close to my same age. They were my besties. Our parents stayed together as a village, moving us around to different small towns between Florida, South Carolina, and North Carolina. Together we played, laughed, swam, sang, played with dolls, chased lizards, rode bicycles, stuck firecrackers in the barks of the trees, and lit them with matches while my daddy supervised.

I truly loved them with all my heart. We never crossed each other, and never played hateful games like some kids did. It was our perfect world. Those were my happy memories of being a kid. When I was with them I felt like an innocent little girl again as I should have been able to feel all along. They made my life complete.

As we grew into teenagers, we climbed taller trees, rode larger horses bareback, and even rode them into the St Johns river–after we had been drinking Boones Farm. We swam in alligator infested waters, and had sleepovers in tents while telling scary stories. We were always getting into trouble, like the time we put dish soap in the filter system of the inground pool at one of their houses.

We frequently talked about what we planned to do when we grew up. My story never changed, I just wanted to leave. I loved them all very much but I had a mission. It was a sacrifice I had to make, though I didn't share with them the reasoning behind my plans. I feel they knew so much more than we ever discussed between us.

There was time I could've allowed someone into my terrors, but I was afraid of the threats. Even the threats from my trip to Atlanta,

Georgia. That trip where I was almost sold to the Colombian Cartel. I never let anyone inside. I kept my distance from anyone getting too close. I simply wouldn't have known where to begin.

I was numb to the love my parents gave me. Inside me lay an unforgiving soul, and self-blame. Shadows of ugly and dirty looked me right square in the face when I graced past a mirror. I was always looking for a way out. Every man who stole my innocence away as a little girl remapped my own self-image and my view of the world around me.

CHAPTER FOUR

Then There Was Kevin

1976-1977 (14 and 15 Years Old)

Kevin had a charm all his own at the age of twenty-eight. Standing tall and proud at six foot-two with sandy brown hair, he carried himself with an air of authority, with his shoulders back and head held high. His eyes could get as dark as the fur on a grizzly bear when he was angry and yet, they could change in an instant to an iridescent olive when he was loving.

He had ended marriages to two very beautiful, strong-minded, college-educated, independent wives. They were not his type; he couldn't control them.

Kevin needed someone who was already crushed, shattered, and living in a semi-state of shock from some traumatic event. He needed a girl who was ready to be completely dependent on him. That was part of his illness. He needed to be solely responsible for turning the ugly duckling into a beautiful swan.

Kevin's looks were mirror images of Easy Rider Peter Fonda and young Robert Redford. His voice was always so soft, quiet, and soothing as well as secretly conniving. He also had that alluring quality of being a bad boy looking for a bad girl. I was, no doubt, ensnared by his well-crafted charisma. The way he would tilt his head slightly forward while gazing at me from the other side of a room made me completely dizzy.

He had just finalized his second divorce when he met me. I didn't really feel so lucky, I only knew that I felt safe. For me, that's all that really mattered. Ex-wife number two would say things to me in front of him. Kevin would call her out, that it was jealousy making her act so rude. The exes were both equally appalled that he was so recklessly dating a school-aged girl. Every time I saw ex-wife number two, I could see her broken heart through her eyes. It always made me sad to think that ex-wife number two still loved him so much.

Kevin was an extraordinarily handsome man. At the time I felt him to be borderline perfect. I was fourteen years old when twenty-seven-year-old Kevin first laid eyes on me. He gently caressed my hair to the side, revealing my baby blues. That's what he always called my blue eyes, except when I cried. Then he told me that he could see the ocean in them. I let him in to see the brokenness, pain, and vulnerability my young soul harbored. I needed him to love me.

Kevin was a motorcycle-riding pedophile, master of his own charm and craft and successful at his own game, no matter the age involved.

I had met Kevin through a mutual friend and he was kind and generous to me from the start. Soon I was spending lots of time at his house, helping him with whatever. I loved working with my hands, being crafty and creative. Before long I was helping him make stained glass pieces. He entrusted me with the glass cutter and diamond bit grinder. I was so excited the first time I ran a bead with the soldering iron. He taught me how to sketch my own patterns and pick out the colors of different glasses. He taught me how to tell which type of glass came from which country.

I had never done any art to speak of. As far as signing up for art classes at school, well, my absences were becoming more and more frequent. It's not that I had lost interest in school, it was because there was never a foundation of interest in the first place. I dismissed the entire thought on a regular basis, it just wasn't meant for me. I had thought, *not now anyway!* I was too busy feeling free and safe in the same breath. As long as I was with Kevin, I was free from pain and no longer a threat to my family's welfare. I thought I must've been doing something right.

Kevin kept me busy by teaching me new things, like polishing the chrome on his bike. *How relaxing!* I thought. I would get lost in perfecting the shine on his bike that I could not accomplish in my own life. I could not buff away my own grime and dirt. I was the happiest of my entire young life. I listened to and loved on his music. Every day that passed, I fell more in love with him. Unbeknownst to me, he was drawing me into his web.

All I ever wanted to do was to please him and make him like me more. I was only a young girl, and incredibly naïve to this man's manipulative ways. I wasn't worried about what I didn't know, he had said that he would teach me everything. I was good with that. I thought he was so handsome, and I was comforted by his soft tone.

At fourteen, I preferred to be with Kevin than anywhere else. We frequently went riding on his motorcycle into the woods near our town to find places to go swimming or to make love on a blanket. In Florida, the swimming holes were plentiful. Far into the woods, where the live oaks canopied the knee-deep crystal-clear creeks, you could hear a dewdrop fall on a leaf far in the distance. There were only sounds of nature for miles around.

Kevin lived in town, only blocks from my parent's house, in an old two-story house. It could barely be seen from the road because of the various overgrown bamboo shoots and palm fronds. The paint was flaking off the exterior of the old house, leaving the surface with speckled off-white and raw wood colors. The entire property was shaded by an array of Florida live oak trees, pecan trees, clumping bamboo, palm trees, and fern that covered the overgrown, un-kept tropical environment that was the backyard.

Kevin thought the house was at least a hundred years old. The interior was no more well-kept than the outside. His furniture was all hand-picked antiques. In the front living room was his Duncan Phyfe sofa, covered with old worn-out upholstery. Next to it was an empty two-foot antique brass artillery shell, turned upright, with a display of dried-out sea oats from the beach, courtesy of me. There was an aged teak bar at the other end of the living room, with different colored wood slates that fanned out its front to create a design. It also had a brass tube footrest that curved around at floor level.

Kevin prized his reel to reel that he kept on top of the teak bar. Every day he played from his collection of 60s and 70s music. I was so intrigued by the whole process of loading the reels. He would put one full reel onto a spindle, then delicately thread the end of the magnetic tape audio recording through the mechanical parts, locking them into place. Then he attached the end of that tape to the empty reel resting on the other spindle. Once in place, he would flip the switch to turn it on.

As the tape fed thru the recorder, such clarity came through his wooden box speakers. The sound was translucent. I closed my eyes and envisioned the musicians sitting there in the front room and jamming with us!

When he got home from work, he loaded his reel to reel, then grabbed a cold one from the old 1930 Monitor Top Refrigerator in the kitchen.

Kevin's only plans were to work construction for the moment to save money for us to leave. He encouraged me to stay in his house during the day while he worked. He told me, "don't worry about school, I'll send you to school once we've moved away. It will all be worked out soon. I promise! I don't want anything standing in our way. I don't want to have to worry about any new little friends, or even boyfriends, so stay here. I will protect you, always."

I would wake up and get dressed and ready for school at my parent's house and go, as instructed by Kevin, to his house for the day.

For me, my life had changed for the better. At fourteen, Kevin claimed me as his own. He was a hero of sorts to a broken, torn, teenaged girl, who was looking for a way out.

CHAPTER FIVE

Chasing Happiness

1976-1977 (14 and 15 Years Old)

Kevin knew I wasn't happy. I tried to show him how happy I was—really, I did. But he told me that he could see inside my soul. He could've told me anything and I would've believed him. I was a walking target. Moving us out of town immediately seemed so important to him and I just went along with whatever he said. He was saving me from my own afflictions. I owed him my life.

Though I never confided my past details to Kevin, he knew that I was a troubled teenager. It seemed to me that the only way I could free myself from my past trauma, was to surrender to the hands of an adult who understood me.

I was lost long before Kevin had celebrated his victory by having his way with me.

At fourteen, he declared to me that I was his. At fifteen, we actively dated and partially lived together at Kevin's house on Lyle Avenue. When I was at my parents' house he was always pulling up at the curb, either on his Harley or in his old truck.

Some of my family members accepted Kevin, while others rejected him. My bestie cousins, who I was closest to, did not accept him at all. As far as they were concerned, he was too old and very controlling. They didn't understand why I couldn't see how manipulative he was. It's true, I didn't see it.

He taught me early on that being respectful was very important in a relationship. That when he spoke I should not waste any time in doing as he asked me to do. That was just part of being *the woman.* So naturally I would jump up right away, just to please him. He would kiss me and tell me I was doing a good job learning how to be a respectful woman.

My cousins desperately tried to talk me out of being his girlfriend. One day I mentioned to Kevin that I missed them. He told me that I shouldn't be around them anymore, that they were jealous of our love and would be out to destroy what we had. That made me sad. I knew he didn't approve of them, and I knew what that meant. I knew I had to choose. I didn't see my cousins for a long time after that.

Their knowledge of my past life was all butterflies and laughter. Apart from those cherished memories, they didn't know the bad things that I had lived through. At least I didn't think they did. I'd never told anyone about my childhood abuses, only that one cousin, Elizabeth, because of her father. And only regarding her father, not about my other abusers.

But now, thinking back, I might have told one of my other cousins, Sara. Sometimes I think that I remember seeing her there too, being victimized at the same time. That may have only been in my dreams, though. She was such a big part of my life.

At times, I believed that a lot more happened than I could even remember. I'd become good at disconnecting from the trauma. I think it was my defenses kicking in. Much like when you go into shock, I suppose. The body knows how much it can handle, and then it just shuts down, stores it away, and forgets it, for the moment.

For most of my childhood through the time I met Kevin, I talked to God a lot. I could feel His supernatural presence following me around, shielding me from most of the bad that *could've* happened to me. Momma always told me that, "If you believe in God, and have faith, and trust, then He will answer your prayers. You will be protected by His grace." I never forgot to ask Him to protect me, but it always seemed to be after I was in distress.

Six months past my 15th birthday, Kevin announced that it was time to approach my parents. I felt secure in Kevin's presence, yet skeptical about leaving my parents. Oddly, he had a way with keeping me mesmerized. I robotically let Kevin orchestrate my life for me.

I agreed to go along with his plan. Kevin promised we could return to Florida anytime I got homesick and wanted to see my family. I was good with it for that reason alone. I knew that it wouldn't take very long for me to begin missing my parents. I loved them so much, along with my entire family, except, of course, for those who had abused me and my cousins. He told me that after we were settled in a house of our own, my parents, siblings, and even my cousins could come out west to visit. That all sounded like a great plan to me!

That is also what he told me that he would say to my parents when he asked the big question, the one that I was certain they would say "no" to. The cascading results of my chasing after happiness, love, and protection landed me in many life-threatening situations. Kevin was there to rescue me for his own wicked purposes and I was a more than willing participant.

CHAPTER SIX

<hr/>

Parental Consent

1977 (15 Years Old)

After painting houses all day in the sweltering heat, my daddy had just finished showering. I could hear my parents discussing their Friday evening plans in the kitchen, as Kevin and I walked through the front door and into the living room.

My sister Bridgette was watching the television while crocheting. She looked up when we came in and said, "Hey guys! What are you up to?"

It was four o'clock and the Gilligan's Island song was playing, "Just sit right back and you'll hear a tale, a tale of a fateful trip, that started from a tropic port, aboard this tiny ship…."

I reached down and gave her a hug while Kevin smiled and patiently waited with his hands slightly dipped into his front pockets. "Nothing much. Just out riding around and getting some fresh air."

Ben, my little brother, was on the floor playing with his matchbox cars. As soon as he saw me, he abandoned his post and jumped up into my arms. "Sissy! I missed you so much! Where were you? Want to play cars with me?"

I knew that I didn't have the time to play at that moment, but I hugged my baby brother close. "Sissy loves you too, Ben! I will play with you later! I promise!"

He seemed content with that and returned to semi-watching tv and playing cars. Standing next to Kevin, I glanced at the TV to see the professor and the captain as they were plotting away and drawing with long sticks in the sand. It was the best plan ever to finally escape that deserted island.

I noticed how my momma and daddy's postures straightened when we walked into the kitchen and they realized that Kevin was with me. It was like he was the Prince of Wales or something! It always amazed me the control he had over people.

My momma spoke up first, offering some sweet tea to Kevin. "Please have a seat. It's so hot outside! Here let me turn that fan on for you."

Kevin always addressed my parents by their first names. "Thank you so much! I do love your sweet tea, Mary! Yes, it is very hot outside. Has been all week! John, it must be hard painting houses this time of the year! Thank you, Mary, the fan feels nice!"

He slowly nursed his iced tea as his eyes peered over the top of the glass. Kevin followed my daddy with his eyes while he took a seat at the other end of the kitchen table.

My daddy easily assured Kevin that his current work was indoors where ACs kept it cool. He asked, "so, Kevin, have you been fishing lately?"

Kevin responded without hesitation, "Not lately, I have been working a lot, and spending my free time teaching Tammie how to make stained glass. Have you gone to any good fishing holes lately?"

One thing my daddy loved *a lot* was talking about fishing, camping, and hunting squirrel or rabbit deep in the Florida woods. "Yeah, I was out at the dam last weekend. Caught us a mess of catfish, my brother James, and me did. But the mosquitos tore us up somethin' good, don't ya know!"

I stood in the kitchen entranceway, where I could see my siblings in the living room and listen to what was being said in the kitchen, while Momma was washing dishes. I frantically searched my mind for a rationale for what I was doing. As the moments ticked by and more trivial chit-chat passed between my daddy and Kevin, I began to doubt my decision. My heart was pattering so fast and sharply that I thought I might have a heart attack right there.

Kevin and I had discussed it several times before braving the trip over to my parents' house, for the big question. But Kevin seemed more sure of himself than me. He acted like it was an easy task and had told me numerous times to stop worrying over it.

Kevin had said to me, "I'll do the talking, but it isn't going to be difficult. They're already letting you date me. You were at my house even before you turned 15 and you practically live with me now. They trust me and they'll let you come with me. Watch me in action!"

I didn't have any input in the discussion. I was more shocked at what I was doing, than excited for it to happen. He already knew of birthmarks that not even my doctor should've known about and I placed all my trust in him. He was truly the established hero of my heart.

For sure, I had wanted to leave home. That had always been my plan. I had to trust him, that he would bring me back when I got homesick.

Just thinking about it, my stomach was making loud noises as it churned from the stress of it all. I already knew that I had no choice but to leave my family to protect them from my cousin's threats! I could hear his voice, "I will find you and beat you and rape you if I want to. If you tell or they find out, I will mess your family up bad!" Those threats followed me throughout my teenaged years.

My momma had gone to the hallway bathroom and now re-entered the kitchen, startling me from behind. I was glad that she didn't sense how nervous and jumpy I was. Kevin kept giving me the eye, which commanded me to calm myself down.

Momma went to the other side of the table and sat between Daddy and Kevin, saying, "You kids have any plans for this evening?"

"*Kids?*" I thought to myself. Even my oldest siblings Caroline and Victor, who were ten and eleven years older than myself, were still two years younger than this man. For that matter, he was only 15 years younger than my mother!

Kevin spoke up, "Yeah, we were thinking about going camping at Blue Oyster Springs for the weekend. There is supposed to be some good ole bluegrass bands there, and I *do love* my bluegrass music. I might even take my banjo. There's always good food at those festivals! We'll probably have some bar-b-que and they're always roasting oysters at those festivals!"

He knew exactly what to say to please my parents as they were absorbed with his presence. *Really Kevin?* I thought. *Going away for the entire weekend? That was not even a request!* He was growing in confidence by the minute! My parents didn't even flinch at what he said.

I glanced over to see Bridgette's expression, from the living room. She looked straight at me with disapproval. She continued listening in on the conversation in the kitchen, but turned her glance back toward the television. I watched as she squinted in disbelief at things that were being said. It was almost like she couldn't believe she was a witness to what was transpiring, all that I was getting away with, at the age of 15!

Momma had moved from her seat to the sink to make a pot of coffee. She said, "well, Kevin, that all sounds like some good times! John and I are getting ready later to go to Captain Moe's and help my sister out with her restaurant tonight."

Kevin's brazen assertiveness was becoming unnerving. "Actually," he said with feigned sheepishness, "there is something I needed to tell you both."

Momma had finished making the coffee and was washing up a few dishes, but she gave a final rinse to a glass, turned off the faucet, and, drying her hands with the kitchen towel she asked, "what is it, Kevin? Is everything okay?"

I couldn't think of what he needed to "tell" them! The previous discussion between us was about requesting permission for me to leave with him. I thought I might be sick. I was secretly doubting my decision and wondering how to get out of it. But at this point it felt like there was no turning back. If I denied him my company on that trip, he may leave for Texas anyway. I would be devastated! If I stayed I would be at risk of being hurt again. Worse yet, if my parents found out about my past trauma, then my cousin's threat would come true and he could turn deadly! Oh, I just couldn't bear the thought of that happening! It would all be my fault!

"Mary and John, Tammie and I eloped last night."

I thought Bridgette might fall right off the couch as she stared straight at me. It was all one huge surprise. I was silently hyperventilating, or maybe just my heart was, or was that my stomach? I panicked. "*Eloped*!?" The conversation had not gone as he and I had planned! "*Eloped*!"

He continued, as his eyes darted from Momma to Daddy. "Of course, if you object we can get it annulled immediately! It's just that I love your daughter so much and I'd never let anything bad happen to her." He leaned forward in his chair in assumed earnestness, "I would really like to have your blessing. Also, I would like to take Tammie with me out to Texas. I promise to take care of her and protect her from harm. I would bring her back if she got homesick, I promise."

At that point, all I wanted was for my parents to object! *Say no!* I pleaded mentally. I was afraid of my own decision-making abilities. I did not have a very good track record there. It wasn't right and I felt it throughout my body.

I was transfixed by his gaze. I knew he was silently commanding me to play along with his story as my parents looked at me from across the room. If only I didn't know what love felt like. I felt sick! Anything left solid in my stomach was becoming pulverized, as I could hear the water shooting from one side of my body to the other.

My parents turned to look at each other in unison. I noticed their glowing skin. Had it been glowing before? The realization of it hit me. *They are proud of me!* They both looked back toward the entrance of the kitchen, at me. I saw tenderness slowly building in their faces.

What I expected from my parents was for them to put their foot down and tell me to go to my room! They were not that kind of parents though. They were tender-hearted, always being loving and wanting me to have whatever it took to make me happy.

Even so, I never expected them to even consider Kevin's original plan, much less this outlandish announcement! From the moment

Kevin and I met, all he talked about was going to Texas. I never saw past those words. To me that's all they were. Just words. I never truly believed he would actually want to leave.

Daddy had a serious glow about him as he looked at me, his youngest daughter. "So, is this what you really want, Pumpkin?" He always called me 'Pumpkin' or 'Sugar.' I cherished the time I spent with that man in the woods and fishing, and didn't even know it at the time. He was such a good daddy.

Time froze and all eyes were on me. Even my sister Bridgette was waiting to hear my response. I suddenly felt like chalk lined my throat, making it difficult to swallow. I felt the membranes in my head swell and squeeze out all the sound! I attempted to speak but failed. I gagged from the chalk. I reached forward and snatched Kevin's big glass of sweet tea out of his mouth and swallowed it as though I were dying of dehydration from weeks in the Sahara Desert.

I cleared my throat and gave Daddy my first answer without thinking. "Yes!" left my mouth before my brain could say 'no.'

"I leave it up to your momma then. If she's happy with it, I am good with it. I give my blessings." He turned the floor over to Momma.

Momma looked at Kevin with more sincerity than I'd ever seen in her tear-filled sweet blue eyes. "Do you promise to make sure she finishes school, and you promise to love her and keep her safe?"

Kevin chirped immediately, "Yes! Mary, I promise!"

Momma finalized the deal with, "then I give my blessings too!"

So, that's it? They now believe that Kevin and I eloped and that I'm literally married to this man! I was half scared to my core, and half lunging into a sea of forgetfulness. It was always easier for me to float to this place of nothingness when the buzzing sounds became too much for my tender heart to bear. I had gone into full-blown shock once again.

He was saying something to my parents about our departure date being in a week. That's all I heard, as I had floated away to some-place else. I wasn't even sure if I'd remembered to say, 'thank you,' 'yay,' or even smile to my parents before we left. Had I hugged anyone or even said good-bye? Kevin guided me outside and he mounted his bike at the curb in front of my parent's house. I stood on the edge of the lawn with only a blank stare. Kevin reached out for my arm and steered me to straddle the bike behind him, lifting each foot onto the pegs. One strong jump on the peddle, and the low rumbling hum came alive beneath us. That bike always reminded me of a caged-up dragon in disguise. He pushed the crank pedal in gently toward the motor with his inner heel. Pivoting back his right hand slightly on the handle, we were off.

We rode slowly down the quiet city streets of my hometown, the low rumble-clunking of the engine echoed off the houses as we coasted passed them. I was in deep thought about nothing. It was as though my capability to acknowledge the world around me had ceased. My life had changed. I stepped into my parent's house a little girl, and out of it as an imaginary wife. I had not an inkling of what just happened. I had not prepared for this. I couldn't even be excited, because I wasn't really married.

Just then, the bike came to a halt at the glass storefront of the ABC store. Kevin smiled down at me as he was standing on the curb by then. "Tammie, I'm going inside really quick to pick up a bottle of wine for us to celebrate! Stay put and watch the bike, we'll be home soon!" He lifted my chin with his two first fingers and planted a gentle and everlasting memory of love on my lips.

Home? Is that what he had just said? To that narrow two story house on Lyle Avenue? The place I'd stayed in for months, was that *my* home now? Officially? I did love that house. Its ambiance seemed so tranquil. It was a historical beacon of the families that inhabited it many years before. From the ceramic bathtub held up by its clawed feet, to the old wood flooring throughout the entire house, to the stained-glass kitchen door that lead out to the yard. There were creeping sounds when I ascended the staircase and, if I dared, the additional steps up to the old musky A-framed attic. On the second floor was our bedroom. *Our bedroom?* The walls had been knocked out to create one large simple room. Against the front wall was our brass bed and, next to it, a single French door lead out to the balcony that faced the street.

We sat on the floor of that balcony many nights before, toking on a weed cigarette. There, with a stillness in the air, we had talked lightly of Texas. With Kevin, even my nightmares had stopped tormenting me. He enabled me to feel. Love rewired me. Beneath my automated actions everything was lucid in love. That love was a river of nutrients feeding my every need and sustaining me in this abyss that had been my life. I was truly in love with this man whose language was hypnotically captivating to my now colorful existence.

Sitting on the bike waiting for Kevin, I took a deep breath in of the fresh night air to revive my senses. I was just going with it, trying to believe that it must be right. There were boxes stacked up against the inside glass of the store, as if they'd just received a new shipment but I could see the top of Kevin's head as he left the register and walked toward the storefront door. Handing me the bag of wine, he slid his leg across and straddled the seat in front of me. Riding toward my new life on the back of Kevin's bike, I thought about this intense love I had for him. Why was I so stunned by the outcome of that conversation with my parents? They did as they thought I wanted them to do. Hadn't they always? *It would be wrong to deny my own self, what I've wanted for my whole life*, I thought. Whatever freedom, love, happiness, and peace had meant, that's what I yearned for more than anything.

Once we pulled the big black bike into the depths of the darkened driveway, he dismounted first. As I swung down from the bike, he pulled me close to himself, and cradled my face in his hands. As he bent down to meet my lips he whispered to me, "I will take good care of you, Tammie. You have my word, and a man's word is his honor! Without my word, I am nothing." That is what he said.

He had told my parents he loved me! Love was a big word for him to use. I would've followed him around the earth and back! Love is the word he used to my parents. He promised me comfort, safety, and some crazy fun idea of going west. I believed every word he said to me. My parents also believed in what he told them of his plans to put me through college, to give me a wholesome life, full of nothing but pure love, and to return if I ever became homesick.

CHAPTER SEVEN

Across the States

1977 (15 Years Old)

The trip out to Texas on the motorcycle was like a dream that belonged to someone else. It was breathtakingly exciting! We headed out of the sunshine state, westbound on I-10. Kevin and I both had handkerchiefs knotted on our heads, with helmets strapped on over them for safety. I anchored my braided ponytail down my back and under my shirt, with an additional handkerchief tied around my neck. The promise of riding in the warm sunshine was as nutritious to my body as every breath I took. We were exuberant and free, having no barriers between us and the world. We were both relaxed in the motion of our travel, just coasting along with the highway beneath our feet, at our own pace, our own schedule.

Kevin had said that he was tired of the 9 to 5 workdays. He had worked for years, holding down a job with an engineering firm. He was against all that the government stood for and policies at state and government levels. It clearly upset him that tax money was removed from his pay checks. He would say, "I worked for that money, not the government!"

He detested paying utility bills and taxes of any kind. He had a dream. He wanted to buy land, grow a garden, and have solar panels and a well. He planned to live on the border of Mexico somewhere in Texas, Arizona or California.

Kevin had no big dreams of becoming rich. He was a simple man with a simple plan to live healthy and carefree on the open plain. He would forbid anyone on his land who wasn't invited, and he did not plan to invite anyone. He wanted to build his own house, while living there on the property. I would get excited when Kevin spoke with passion about what he wanted to do. I couldn't wait to help make it come true for him. All I wanted was to make him happy by following him and living out his dreams with him.

At the beginning of the road trip, I kept nudging Kevin to please stop for rest breaks. I didn't mean to be a pain. I needed to stretch my legs every hour or two. The hardtail frame on Kevin's bike receives its name from the lack of rear suspension. The axle is mounted directed on the frame. At least that is what he had said to me. I had ridden enough horses to know what it felt like to be "sore in the saddle." I became sore in my saddle immediately. My legs were like rubber by the time I dismounted that dragon!

The ride was taxing on us both; it was a tremendous strain for the body to get used to. Kevin said that we would eventually get used to it and it wouldn't be so uncomfortable anymore. I sure couldn't wait until that time came! After three days, though, we were both worn out and needed a couple of days to rest our tired bodies.

That third evening there seemed to be no campgrounds for miles, but we kept watching for camping road-signs. It was a clear night, and the temperatures were perfect for pitching a tent. Finally, Kevin slowed the bike down at a deserted exit with no signs of life nor lights anywhere.

He pulled off the highway into a random corn field. Turning off the head lamp, he guided the bike further into the field. The ground was moldable rich soil. Kevin flattened it out to form a bed and there we pitched the red, two-man tent. The full shine of the moon made it possible to see what we were doing as we set up camp for the night. In that field, we were surrounded by mature eight-foot tall corn plants. Kevin had demolished an entire section of those plants, for our camp. I was pretty sure that we weren't allowed to do that but I felt safe with Kevin's choices. After all, it was more dangerous to be driving on the highway tired. That was Kevin's logic.

The crickets were so loud I could hardly think. But that was okay as it drowned out the sound of passing cars in the distance. We laid our heads down and both sighed at the same time, then laughed, knowing we were both spent!

The most perfect existence, I thought. Sleep couldn't have come too soon, for we had been on that Harley for way too long!

Sometime in the night a torrential downpour began beating puddles into the roof of our tent. We both pretended to ignore those marble-sized drops of rain. My brain was moaning, *Not now! We are still so tired!* Suddenly the little red tent collapsed. That moldable rich nutrient soil took on another form: a soft thickened-butter mud.

Scrambling to get out of the flooded tent was a challenge, since it was now just a mass of canvas and tent poles. Every time I stood up to move, the slippery mud yanked my foot out from under me. I was a muddy mess! Our eyes strained to see what was what in the pitch black stormy night.

"Tammie, take this blanket and get on the bike!" Kevin yelled through the thunderous noise.

As we both mounted the motorcycle, Kevin pulled the green tarpaulin over us and the bike. He had also fished out the sopping wet pillows from inside the tent, finding a plastic bag to wrap over them, and scrunched them up as a heap in front of me over the gas tank. Being in the front I leaned over and hugged the pile of plastic covered pillows and blankets, and Kevin snuggled up behind me, as best as he could. Thank goodness it was a warm night, since we were both drenched. The relentless thunderstorm beating against the tarp came in roaring waves. Hovering over the gas tank that night was uncomfortable, but it worked. We slept on an off for the rest of the early morning hours.

Daylight shone through the tarp, as the saturated environment made the air sticky. There were sounds of flies and other insects buzzing in the distance, crows squawking, and a dog barking far away. Coming out from underneath the waterproof cloth, the world resembled a war zone. There lay our red tent, flattened and with thick streaks of mud and debris. We found each other's glance, shaking our heads and half smiling at how we were both covered with mud. With every step we took, we had to fight to pull our feet from the sucking mud. Rolling up the tent, blankets, and pillows as best we could, we rubber-hook strapped it all to the bike.

Kevin and I managed to push the bike out of that horribly muddied cornfield. The motorcycle was covered with mud just like us. Once on solid ground, Kevin gave one pump of his right heel and the motor came alive, creating that clunking, rumbling sound.

Sitting high on the rear seat, I reclined back against the cushion of the sissy bar. We rode off at a slow pace at first, as clumps of mud were flying everywhere! I could feel my skin tightening, as the wind began to dry the fresh mud.

Pulling off at the next exit was a must. We didn't even have shoes on! Just like the exit before, there were no cars or stores, only deserted lush farmland. Kevin pulled off the side of the road and we fished through one of our bags for socks and shoes, pulling them onto our dried feet. And then, there on the side of the road far from civilization, we two filthy, muddy, worn out, tired biker people, brushed our teeth. I felt a new kind of resilience as we stood there, brushing in silence. We stuffed all our things back into the duffle, and we were off again.

CHAPTER EIGHT

Biker's Style

1977 (15 Years Old)

We had been back on I-10 for an hour that morning when we crossed over into the state of Mississippi. Kevin began down shifting on the gears as we approached a small bridge. He had good instincts on finding bridges to drive the bike under though he was never 100% sure it was ever safe and it was a daring venture indeed. He pulled over and told me to get off and walk behind him. I followed as he turned the bike right into the outer bend of the guard railing, down and around the slope of the land to get underneath the bridge. There it was, glassy two-foot-deep see-through water, with a sandy bottom, and a white sand landing. It was absolute paradise with beautiful lush green grass! Kevin made a comment on how, if he had known about this place last night, we would still be sleeping, dry and mud-free. As it was, we used this haven to regroup from our horrible experience the night before.

The traffic flow was minimal, on the bridge above us. It didn't matter anyway; Kevin said no one could see under there. We rinsed the mud from our bedding and tent in the mild current, then wrung them out and laid to the side.

We laid down on the sandy bottom, clothes on, so the current could melt the dried dirt from our skin and clothes. Next, we took out the shower bag, pulled out the soap and shampoo, and began washing in the brisk water, watching the suds flow quickly downstream. Bathing outside had a fascinating element of being in the wild. It was so refreshing, especially because we were so dirty. It was like taking off an extra layer of skin! Our duffle bags were all waterproof, so we pulled out some clean clothes to wear for the day.

The temperature was already rising so we gathered up our wrung-out bedding and dirty clothes, rolled up our tent, and tethered everything tightly to the bike's rear luggage rack. The rack was small, but the tall sissy bar allowed for stacking. Kevin guided the bike slowly up the incline alongside the bridge, as he gave it gas. I followed by foot to the top and we were soon on the road again. Being free from dried mud felt rejuvenating!

Early on, he had advised me to keep my skin covered from the harmful effects of the sun. I could see why he would feel that way, since his mom's skin had turned to leather from years of laying out in the California sun. Kevin kept me supplied with long-sleeved cotton button-up chambray shirts for riding in the harsh rays.

We rode for the next two hours, until Kevin found an exit with a laundromat. He left me there to officially wash and dry our clothes and blankets that had only been rinsed in the water streams underneath the bridge that morning. Kevin gave me exactly enough change for the job and checked in on me periodically.

I could look out the window and see Kevin across the street, at a nearby store. A group of bikers were keeping him company while he sprayed the bike off with a water hose that had been stretched around from the backside of the store. Once, when he checked in on me and brought me a cup of hot tea, he told me that the bikers were also heading west, and that they would be riding with us.

I sat and contemplated my new life while sipping the hot tea. I wondered how my family was, and if any of them were wondering how I was doing too. I missed playing cars with my little brother, making him peanut butter and jelly sandwiches, and singing to him. I remembered playing one last time with him, just before I left. I asked myself, *would he even remember at five years old what I last said to him? Would he remember that I was going away on a trip and that I would be back in a while?* He had asked me what that meant. I really didn't know how to tell him that I didn't even know myself. I just loved on him, and hoped that he'd remember me.

I also sat thinking about my parents and how they always joked around and were always laughing. Momma always had the record player on. I could recall what her album covers looked like; Merle Haggard's "Today I Started Loving You Again," or Tammy Wynette's "Stand By your Man," or Loretta Lynn's "You Ain't Woman Enough to Take my Man."

My momma had often tried to talk to me and get me to confide in her. Telling them about those deep dark secrets of childhood trauma was like trying to speak a foreign language that I didn't know. My parents tried to reach me through gifts. But the horses they gave me didn't produce any confessions. However, those horses did always bring me a sense of peace, especially Champ, the paint horse, with different-colored eyes, one brown and the other light blue. I found peace just brushing his hair, walking him in the yard by the bridle and rein, and riding him, bareback or with a saddle. He was a mean-spirited horse that liked to crow hop, so it took a while before we finally connected. Sometimes I would just sit with him in the pen, and he would reach down and smell my hair. I felt comforted by Champ.

Momma told me that they'd never seen me so happy as when I was with Kevin. The age difference never mattered to them. It was a cultural thing within their generation, or within their own culture. After all, there was a seven-year age gap between my parents. To them, their daughter's happiness was their priority. In my parents' minds, they were doing right by letting me go.

They felt safe with Kevin taking me away. They knew of his family's local business on the other side of town. My older siblings knew him since he was just two years older than them. Knowing that my parents wouldn't be sad and sorry they let me go, somehow made me feel better about leaving.

But I still had to push them out of my mind since the thought of them was causing my stomach to churn with an emptiness no amount of food could satisfy. I was convinced I would see them again, and soon.

I thought of the distance we were riding. I didn't know Texas was so far away. I was beginning to wonder how difficult it would be to get back if I wanted to see my family for the day. Kevin had said he would get me home if I was homesick, but home was getting further and further away by the day.

As I looked over at Kevin I could see the biker women who were gathered there. I had seen biker girls before and they had creeped me out and they smelled like sweat. They wore thick layers of makeup, hip huggers, and halter tops, and no bras. Kevin had told me he liked the way I dressed, sort of like a cowgirl.

He didn't like for me to wear makeup, which was fine for me since I didn't even know how to apply it. He said that "those kinds of women, the ones who wear see-through halter tops, heavy makeup, and never take baths, are loose and trashy." He also told me that dressing like a cowgirl would keep anyone from bothering me or looking at me.

When we stopped just before nightfall that first night with the bikers, we set up camp and ate as a group. We cooked on the grill over the fire and, after our stomachs were filled and tents were all pitched, someone pulled out a guitar and others joined in singing. Kevin let me have a beer or two. He also drank, but not much. He said it wasn't a good idea to lose control around that group.

The biker girls, on the other hand, were full steam ahead and completely out of control. They became belligerently mouthy with each other, as they were guzzling down beer after beer.

With the crackling of the fire, the bikers all laughed and joked loudly, using foul words I had never heard before. Kevin never left my side and it felt good knowing he was always keeping me safe, just as he told my parents he would.

I was stunned that the girls acted so vulgar toward each other. One of them threw a fist at the other and I heard a smack as it made contact with a face. They both dove into each other, kicking up dirt and dust, while screeching like wild animals. They were pulling each other's hair out, slapping in a blinded fury, and attempting to claw each other's eyes out, crying all the while.

All the other bikers were laughing and cheering them on, like it was great entertainment. But it made my heart race, thinking something bad was about to happen to one of them. A nose was bloodied, and the guys decided to break it up.

Kevin took every teaching opportunity. "And that is why I don't let you talk to them. They are always just about to spiral out of control!"

We didn't ride with that group again. A couple of days later, we hooked up with a different group but not for long. We never got attached, nor even knew them by their first names. He felt that riding across country as part of a group made it safer if something went wrong, like if the bike stalled out, got a pinched vacuum line, or a ground cable went bad. Kevin was always on top of things.

He made sure that I was cared for physically. He kept me on a specially-selected vitamin regimen. He started me on them even before I turned 15. He had kept them at his house and made sure I took them when I came over.

He occasionally allowed me to buy a box of color for my hair. He would provide clothes for me thru second hand shops along the way during our journey out west. Kevin didn't feel it was necessary for me to have money. He bought me what I needed. He said that if I wanted something more, that he would make that final decision for me. He asked if that was okay with me, but explained that it was better that way, since we had limited space and all. Oh, I didn't care, I trusted him with my life! He could have it whatever way he wanted as long as he loved me. That's all that mattered.

He persistently reminded me that I wasn't to speak to anyone, especially men. He didn't want me to have any conversations. I could say hello and smile and that was all. He convinced me that everyone wanted to steal our love away.

I believed him.

CHAPTER NINE

Control to the End

1978 (almost 16 Years-Old)

Heading westbound on I-10, I listened to the constant whine of the wind in my ears as I sat on that clunking, roaring Harley beast. My mind was settled into a state of deep tranquility. I looked down at my cupped hands as they lay between us as we rode in the explosive wind. I drifted away into memories of childhood.

I was in a happy place, running through the woods with my cousins. We were barely nine years old. They had come up from Hollywood, FL, for a spring break camping trip. We were at a campground on the edge of the Ocala National Forest. Most of us had tents, but a few family members had small campers. Everyone was settling in, as most of them hadn't seen each other in some time. This spring break trip was an unofficial family reunion. The women were preparing dinner, as the men readied their gear to go fishing the following morning.

The temperature was perfect. The water in the glass gallon jars was already tinted from the tea bags as they seeped in the late afternoon sun. The smell of the popping fire and fog-like smoke lingered in the wooded trails. Sweet familiar laughter echoed through the air, the voices of loved ones would remain for years as peaceful memories, to the younger generation. Their love and honor for God was as firm as their solid foundations they lived.

I don't remember any words that were spoken between my cousins and me, only that intense feeling of freedom as we ran bountifully laughing through those shaded woods. I saw my Hollywood bestie cousins very little and I was overjoyed to see them!

I sat paralyzed as my memories passed in slow motion before me. That was true childish love, untouched by the outside world. Our innocent freedom was like that of an eagle swooping down across a vast serene canyon.

My cupped hands faded back into my vision, but I still sat thinking of my family, my memories, and their value. I wondered what Kevin would say if I told him how real my homesickness already was, after only fifteen days. Would he turn around and take me back home, as promised?

Riding on the open road was a lot like watching a sleepy movie. After a while, my eyelids grew heavy and my body relaxed. I'd sink into a tired dreaminess making me fear I might fall off the bike. Then I'd press closer into Kevin with my arms wrapped around his body, and my chin resting on his shoulder. I could see him smiling at me in the tiny side-view mirror, strangely secured on its thin pedestal, next to his gloved hand. My eyes would map every detail of his long strong arm, with its fine sandy-colored hairs.

When Kevin decided that we needed a rest, he would pull off the road and find some shaded trees. He would take the screened canvas hammock from the bike, and unroll it. Finding two trees, he would suspend the hammock tightly. Once up, we'd crawl inside.

Zipping up the screen to keep out the flies and mosquitos, we would take some of the most delicious naps!

There were times that my body felt sore and just worn out. I didn't mind it so much, it was like living someone else's dream. I loved the adventures that came with riding the open road and seeing our beautiful country.

But I always drifted back to thinking of my family. As the time rolled forward and the weeks fell away behind us, I missed them more and more. I knew they had said they loved me. I could recall details about each of them, their laughter, their voices, and their funny ways.

I began asking Kevin about the possibility of going home to visit them. His answer was always the same: "Not now. Maybe later." My heart ached to at least hear their voices. I asked to call them.

But that's when Kevin began to change. He would bark at me, "No, I'll tell you when you can call them. Don't ask again!"

I had a lot of lessons to learn in my life ahead. Riding on the back of that bike didn't give me a lot to do but sit, think, and view the scenery. That was pleasing enough to me, and my love for nature and the outdoors grew even deeper. That life suited me. I was safe, for now.

I was safe, except when I mentioned my family. Kevin began scaring me a little, but one day I fired back with a bit of attitude. I wanted to see them! They were my parents! It seemed to put fire in his eyes and voice, and his posture stiffened with his lips. I really wanted to go home at that point, no matter the fun I was having. The more I had to ask the more desperate I got for a real answer. I had changed. I had grown up some. I thought that I could live without them, but the reality was that I wanted to go home. I really missed my cousins too.

On that specific afternoon we'd pulled into a campground with a group of Harley riders. Everyone had made camp for the evening. They all busied themselves with different things going on. Some were working on getting a fire started, getting logs for seats set up, polishing bikes, brushing their teeth off in the distance, and hanging something wet on a rope strung between two trees.

I courageously and softly broached the subject with Kevin. "Please, can I at least call them? I really want to go home. If it's the money, I'm sure they'll find a way to wire it, so I can take a bus home. I just miss them so much." I was teary-eyed and began trembling. "I appreciate this trip, really, I do. Thank you. I'm sorry, Kevin, but all I really want now is to just go home! I want to see my parents." The growing anger in his face was changing my concern to fear.

Before I knew it, he had raised his hand and hit me on top of my head, my arms flew up in defense.

He spoke with a controlled, stern tone, "You know what? I've had about enough of this crap from you! You're acting like a piece of shit, you know that? With all I've done for you and that little family of yours! It's time for you to grow up and get over it! You're not going home to mommy and daddy! Your home is with me now! You will learn to do as I tell you to, do you understand me? You will do things my way, or you can just hit the road right now on foot! Without money, without anything! You have lost your rights! Your family gave you away! You're nothing without me! I don't want to hear another word about them! Do you understand me? Answer me right now!"

I was humiliated and filled up with deep sorrow as I felt all the blood leave my face. As I tilted my head down to backhand caress the tears from my eye, I glanced over, realizing the stares we were getting from the entire camp! Tucking my chin down to hide myself, I turned my head to look all the way around me. All the bikers, stopped in silence and watched. No one said a word. I didn't blame those scaredy-cat people for not defending me against this crazed maniac. This was my own battle to get though.

I looked back up to where Kevin waited, keeping my chin lowered in shame. He was still standing at attention, chest out like a rooster with his feathers ruffled up ready for a cock-fight. He was staring down at me, waiting for my answer.

"Yes, Kevin, I understand," I whimpered defeatedly.

As much as Kevin attempted to instill fear in me, I still wanted my parents no matter what he said. He bent down to me as he lifted up my chin, planting a kiss ever so softly onto my lips, and said, "You know, I love you and I am only trying to protect you, Tammie.

I don't want anyone to ever hurt you again. We are married, and your place is with me now."

That proclamation of marriage alone somehow made me blush. He was willing to live in a pretend world with me.

He showed me how to live a care-free life. Many adventures continued on our journey through the states. We stopped in many towns where he'd find a contractor job and work for several days, and then move on to the next town. I saw a lot of different people and stayed in a lot of different places.

On one hand, he made me think there was nothing he wouldn't do for me. Then the other side of him would emerge. He told me not to misbehave, not to ask for anything that I didn't need, including "that family of yours." I knew what he meant. It was easy to understand his meaning when he backed his words up with beatings and emotional scars.

I was alone most of the time when we were stopped for him to work. I was not allowed to leave, not even for a walk. He brought me books to keep me busy. That was all I had: novels, encyclopedias. The books were all used, and he had no problem leaving them when we moved on. One day he came back with my first daily journal. He wanted me to begin writing every day and at every day's end he wanted me to read to him what I wrote.

I wrote in that black five-by-seven log book every day. Kevin gave me a fresh one every year to write my thoughts in. He encouraged creativity, telling me that this was me going back to school. *His* school. He wanted me to write about things that I did, places we went, and my feelings about the environment. There was one page per calendar day and I continued filling them up as we traveled from place to place. A lesson I'd learned the hard way was that I couldn't write anything bad in them. I couldn't talk about any of the abuse.

He always read what I wrote in my journals. I had no privacy growing up under Kevin's control. So, I wrote what I thought he wanted to hear. I'd read it to him as instructed, and he would start getting mad at me without fail.

He would ask "why is there nothing about our love written in your journal today? Isn't that why we have the books in the first place? Now, go sit down in there and write what I told you to! Thoughts of love and happiness, so you'll have something to read to me later, when I ask again! Don't leave anything out! Write how you still love me as your one and only, and how happy our life is together!"

His words would scrape down my throat like a brush on a long stick, getting shoved up and down, scrubbing away at the tender surface, leaving just the raw acid feeling down deep inside my stomach.

We had left Florida by motorcycle, making it all the way to west Texas. Eventually making our way back to Florida a few months later. We were to stay in Florida for two weeks.

Arriving back in our hometown, he allowed me to go see my family. Once. I called to let Momma know that the next day I would be over to see them, but that I wouldn't be able to stay for long. That next morning, he told me to go visit them but to be back in 45 minutes because he had plans for us that day. He said that I could go back the next day.

"Don't be late," was the last thing he said to me.

I was so happy to see my family that I concealed my distress from the past three months of not seeing or speaking to them. They told me that I looked healthy and happy, and that they were very proud of me. I held onto those words long after I waved goodbye to my loving family.

We stayed at Kevin's parent's beach house for the next three days, then returned to his parent's house in town for the rest of that first week. It was only a couple of miles from my parent's house, but I wasn't allowed to return to them that next day, as he had promised. In fact, I didn't get to return at all that trip. I tried peacefully to defend my case, but fear silenced me. I felt I would only make things bad for myself. He had said to me before, "you will never amount to anything if you go back there to stay. Just go ahead, see for yourself!"

I didn't want to fail. I didn't want him to be right. It wasn't as though he didn't make me happy, sometimes.

After that, we moved on to his grandparent's house, for another week. That was an hour drive from my family. There is where we remained until we headed back toward Texas.

Though he discouraged interactions between me and his family, he spoke to them about me, referring to me as his "broken flower." Most of the time I could hear them from the other room. His mother gave her own opinions regarding the "child" he had with him. He responded with discontentment and disputed that he was doing "nothing wrong!" He told her to mind her own business. She didn't express her opinion again that trip.

I thought the way Kevin treated me was normal. He compared it to how a parent would reprimand their kid.

I never wore it as abuse. I accepted it as my life.

As the months turned into a year, the memory of my parents, siblings, cousins, aunts, uncles, and even childhood friends began to fade, like a worn dollar bill in circulation for many decades. I could no longer hear their voices in my memory.

When I stopped crying for them, he saw it as a milestone. It was a sign that I'd finally come to my senses. By this time, I was no closer to understanding how to think for myself. I was sixteen years old. He had cut me off from my family, and they heard nothing from me.

That is, until the camper incident...

CHAPTER TEN

Camper Incident

1979 (Almost 17 Years Old)

Kevin had always told me that he had to *teach me* how to be respectful to him. I would never have done anything to hurt him. In my dependent state of mind, I loved him. Then again, what did I know about love? I was only a sixteen-year-old child at the time.

As time passed the physical abuse became unbearable. Each time he would say that it was my fault that he hit me because I was not listening when he spoke. He had to teach me because I was still young and needed to learn the right way. To overcome each assault, I willed the memory of it to blow away in the wind.

A year after our first return to Florida we were living in a camper at the only campground located in an old west Texas town. We had been in Texas for a year and that's how long it had been since I'd seen my family.

Carrie and Liam, the owners of the property, were a retired couple. They ran the campground and lived at the main house, which was also the welcome center. The campground was small and quaint, with only about twenty permanent residents. Carrie often asked me to join her on a horseback ride. I always declined, knowing Kevin didn't want me out of the camper while he was at work. His logic never made any sense to me. He had no reason to mistrust me but

I sometimes thought it had to do with his idea that everyone was as devious as he was. He still was of the mindset that everyone was out to destroy our love. He was probably afraid that someone would try and snatch me away from him; he trusted me with no one. Having sat inside that camper month after month, never going anywhere all day long, I was growing restless. So, one day, when she asked me, I felt I had earned the right to go out riding. That rule of his, to stay inside the camper, was an old one. So, while Kevin was at work, I readily agreed that it was a great day for it!

Carrie and I were out for a few hours, riding across the barren desert. I had enjoyed horseback riding throughout my childhood. I thought I had experienced the best in riding, but this trail ride proved me wrong. The weather was perfect with crisp, clean air, coupled with that earthy smell that only the desert carries. *It's straight out of a western movie,* I thought. Carrie had even given me a pair of leather cowboy boots and hat to wear for the ride. I was lifted to a new sense of identity.

Carrie was a smoker, and kept offering me a cigarette every time she lit up. Now, I already knew that Kevin detested cigarettes in a red-hot way, calling it a "filthy and toxic habit." His mother had always smoked. He had said that she was a beautiful woman when she was young, but between cigarettes and the sun, her looks were ruined forever!

However, I was thinking like a sixteen –about to be seventeen– year-old young lady. I was truly lost in the cowgirl-riding-horses-in-the-desert moment. I was living out my happy day while laughing, getting fresh air, and conversing with *someone.* We rode alongside the cactus and sage bushes, as the hooves were clacking on the white rocky desert floor. The ride ended, and Carrie offered me a late lunch. I declined and told her that I needed to get to my chores and start dinner.

Laughing in her light-spirited way, she said it was fine, and that next time I could help her put the horses away. I was already excited about the next time we were going riding!

Thinking of how I wanted to share the story of my day with Kevin, I was elated from the day's adventure. Back at the camp area,

I had successfully arrived with plenty of time left before Kevin got home. Dusty dried sweat covered me with glistening salt crystals and the smell of saddle oil, as I hummed a song that I'd heard on the radio in the horse stall, "don't it make my brown eyes blue." As I began quickly gathering my things to go to the shower house, I heard the Harley pull up outside. *Oh my*, I thought. *He's home!*

My mind started racing. I thought I felt my heart skip a few beats, then accelerate. I thought I was old enough to make decisions about riding horses! I was straining to recall my day and if I could be in trouble for anything! Why was he home so early? Surely, he wouldn't get mad at me for riding!

Kevin was now thirty, and his past rage with me had been tamed for a month or so. It was difficult to know when he would turn cruel again. It was even harder to know exactly what would set him off. That thought was always lingering since Kevin was hot-tempered! His strength had already been proven to me. He had only recently told me to behave when he was away at work, and not to leave the camper. Then I panicked further, *Oh no!* I was mistaken. It wasn't an old rule after-all. *What have I done now?* He had massive abilities to inflict pain. I was beyond terrified. I pulled myself into a trap of fear that worsened with each additional tick of the clock. I was unable to conceal my horror. I realized, with deep seated-terror that, for whatever reason, I was going to be in trouble for *something*.

The camper we lived in was an old converted bread truck. A year before, Kevin had worked for weeks getting it ready for the westbound trip from Florida. The camper was compact living quarters without a bathroom. There was a bed that converted from the booth table. He had built kitchen cabinets with a kitchen sink and drain, small fridge, and a stove top that came from another camper. There was one way into the camper, and one way out. The back door—normally available for loading and unloading the Harley during traveling—had been blocked off with a table.

Kevin stepped onto the platform outside, which was an old wooden pallet that served as our porch. My heart pounded so loudly against the wall of my chest that I barely heard him enter. Dizzy with worry that I was about to be assaulted and beaten by him I immediately felt a dark cloud of guilt and shame. My teeth clenched, and I began trembling. I saw the power building as his eyes flamed with anger.

It was one o'clock; he normally got home at five. No dinner, *and* the bed was still unmade from the morning! I was filthy! Just then I realized with an even deeper sense of horror, I didn't even have enough time to de-fumigate! The look on his face told me that he knew right away that I'd been smoking cigarettes. The odor was a lingering noxious cloud. Even I could still smell it on myself. He had to see the look of terror on my face! I stood before him, coated in a blanket of shame. I was caught red handed, doing the unthinkable. In Kevin's psychotic world there were consequences for going against his rules. Smoking carried a heavy sentence, and I knew that I was in big-time trouble.

He seemed to focus in on that very thing the minute he entered the camper. This was his palace, where he considered himself master and where no one else had any rights.

He started out with "so what man did you go bumming ciga-rettes from, huh? You know that you are *NOT* permitted to smoke! *NOT* permitted to leave this camper! *NOT* permitted to talk to *any-one* while I am at work!"

I tried to explain where I had been, "Kevin, there weren't any men. It was Carrie, the owner's wife, I went riding horses today. I didn't do anything wrong, Kevin, I would never…"

His lips curled in tightly and his chest pushed out firmly as though he were posing for some weight lifting photo. He spoke in a monotone, creepy, controlled voice, "I don't remember giving you PERMISSION to open that door! Haven't I told about leaving this camper when I am at work?! You DID NOT have permission to be riding any horses! You will NEVER have permission to ride any horses again! EVER! DO you understand me?"

I kept thinking to myself, *these were not old rules and I thought it was okay.*

I knew from previous physical assaults from him what it meant when his eyes became wild with evil. It meant that the person inside had checked out and he was void of human compassion. His words came like daggers, striking me in the heart with every syllable as he was working himself up for the physical attack to follow.

"Please Kevin, I didn't mean to go against what you said, I'm so sorry, I'm not a bad person, I promise to never..."

He stopped me mid-sentence.

He swayed forward and slammed me on the top of the head. I yelped out in pain. He spoke with mouth barely open through his unnaturally thinned lips, "*Shut up*, right NOW! *Shut your mouth*! DO you hear me?"

I muffled my own sobs, and tried pleading with my eyes for him to stop. "Why do you think I leave this camper every day?! To go partying somewhere? No! It's to put food in your stomach! A roof over YOUR head! You ungrateful *bitch*!" He started punching me again, this time with his other hand, on the side of my head. He continued throwing daggers of words, with spit spewing from his mouth.

Every blow to my head sent a bolt of lightning through me, and my stomach churned with nausea. I tried to resist and pleaded desperately for him to stop.

"Please, you're hurting me, Kevin, you're hurting me bad." I threw up my arms every chance I could to defend against the blows. But he kept moving and holding my arms away, as his target was my head.

"*Shut UP* I said!" I heard another *whoosh* and blacked out.

He was still yelling at me and thrashing like a madman when I came to. I was without a shelter in his storm. I knew it was not possible to stop his forward momentum, as he always managed to convince himself that I had stepped over some Kevin-appointed line. He was convinced that I wanted some other man besides him. There was no escaping his fatal intentions. He had lost all reason and wanted to kill me. I was now backed into the depths of his animal cave. He was hitting me all over my head.

At some point, I wasn't sure if he was still speaking through those tightened lips of his, but I knew that he was hitting me. Electric lights flashed through my head with each assault. Everything inside my head was on fire! Loud buzzing sounds pounded my head. The image of the room faded out.

He added pain to my wounds with his fresh daggers of words. "I will teach you a lesson to not listen to me…if I have to beat you…." I saw the blow coming then heard it like a 12-gauge shotgun, the sound was a deafening explosion inside my head. In slow motion, he faded away again.

I remembered waking up to him being on top of me. I couldn't breathe and was having flashbacks to when I was being violently raped by my cousin at twelve, I began fighting him off. His breath was heavy on my face. He swung and hit my ear and the explosion was more intense than before. The sound numbed everything, as the world went black again.

The abuse had gone on for a while even after I fainted, for when I came to blood crusted my entire face. He had split the skin in areas on my head, and my hair was matted with blood. My injuries were so bad that I could see only white specks floating in my vision. It took a few seconds to pass the white speck stage, so that I could see clearly enough to realize he was gone. I heard the Harley start up; and I pulled myself up to the counter just in time to see him drive away down the boulevard. There on the table was a pan of dirty water with a floating dingy colored wash cloth. On the floor in a pile was a towel and his dirty clothes. He had washed up before he left, knowing I was lying unconscious from him beating me 'til I was nearly dead. The psychotic lunatic was no medic, there was no way to know if I was okay. He had left me there alone on that bed to die!

As disoriented as I was, I knew that I had to respond to save my own life. There was blood everywhere, on the sheets, on the mirror behind the bed, underneath my fingernails. My head hurt so badly. The pounding was in rhythm with my heartbeat. I gathered my things for a shower.

As quickly as I could without passing out or staggering like a drunk, I made my way to the bath house. I was on a mission. First, I needed to get the stench of him off me as fast as I could. That was my priority before leaving for good. Leaving was the only thing I had left to do. There was no point in believing he would not beat me to a pulp again and succeed in killing me next time.

With the water on as hot as I could stand, it seemed to not only melt away the aches and pains but to quell the nausea in my gut. I winced as the steaming hot shower stung my scalp. I began cleansing the dust, dried sweat, and blood, and whatever else came from Kevin off my body. There was no amount of soap that could erase the terror and hurt that lay shivering beneath my soul on that day. That filth had penetrated deep into every layer of my mind and body. I was weakened by Kevin's assaults. He had left me there *to die*. I wanted nothing more to do with him. The more I thought about it, the angrier I got. All over smoking cigarettes and riding horses! He had left me covered in shame, and I knew that to him, I was lower than dirt. I had lost everything: my honor, my dignity, and my dream of us! 'Us' was no more. However painful it was, I had to will myself forward and never look back!

I bathed with determination. My hands reached out to walls that seemed to be rotating. I was unsteady on my feet, disoriented, and at times ready to spin out of control. My head had almost stopped bleeding, but the pounding was getting worse, and it was making me nauseated. I stood under the running water trying to wash the blood from my hair. I was scared that Kevin would return before I could finish. The nausea was worsening, but I ignored it. I had to calm the rising panic inside me. It was *time* to define myself and make a stand for my own life. If I stayed, I would end up dead.

I dried myself off while walking to the dressing bench and sat down. I dried some more. I felt as though the warm shower water were still trickling down through my hair but I wasn't sure what was wrong. The walls began bending and the world became fuzzy and disoriented. That's when the blood began trickling down my face and I blacked out.

When I woke up I was stretched out on the cold concrete tile, and I was lying in vomit. I reached up to touch my head and there was still some fresh blood. I knew that I needed to apply pressure. I had to stay seated for a few minutes, despite the putrid vomit covering my face and chest.

I held pressure on my head with that blood-stained towel for three minutes, and I counted every second. I couldn't wait anymore.

I quickly washed off again, dried off with my dirty clothes, and dressed. Grabbing all my things, I left the bathhouse. Even though I was dizzy, and my head was pounding out of control, I walked purposefully, knowing my life was in danger. I returned to that camper. I threw all that would fit into a bag and zipped it up. Then I walked gingerly across the paved area, over to the campground's front office.

"Please, may I use your phone?"

Carrie turned and saw me standing at the front desk. "Oh, my dear little friend, Tammie, what has happened to you?" I still had dried blood on my pale white skin, and some swelling to my brows. My eyes were bloodshot red. Except for the blood, I looked as though I'd just taken a shower and had been crying a lot. Kevin had always hit me in the head, where my hair covered the evidence. That's just how he did things.

I stood before my friend speechless, hungry, beaten, nauseated, afraid, bewildered, and in excruciating pain. I was tired of being a punching bag for a deranged madman. I never deserved his beatings or the way he spoke to me like I was garbage.

I was emptied out of who I was and the person I had allowed him to make me sickened me. I could not have been more lost and alone. Yet my spirit rose to the occasion, and I became sound-minded enough to know that I was leaving him. It didn't matter that my family lived half-way across the states. If I didn't want to die, I needed to leave right then!

Still, I was in shock. As I stood before my friend, I repeated myself like a mechanical robot, "Please, may I use your phone."

Carrie looked at me, "Honey, who did this to you?" She called out to her husband to call the police. "Are you hurt? Were you physically assaulted? This is *bad*, Tammie! No one deserves this, honey. It just isn't right! What was he thinking beating up on you like this? Has it happened before? He needs to be locked up. He is a dangerous man! Tammie, where is he?"

"No, you can't call the police! I only want to leave. He will come find me and kill me. I'm afraid for my life. I just want to get out!" I responded sternly. "It was Kevin. I'm only telling *you*, but I will deny it if you call the police on him. I just want to leave and be gone, forever."

Carrie looked at me, then at her husband. She asked Liam to go put on some water for tea and he disappeared through the doorway behind the desk, to their adjoining house.

"Here, you need to come into the house until we figure this out, in case he comes back."

She guided me through the doorway, following Liam into their kitchen. Carrie handed me an icepack from the freezer for my head and Liam set a cup of hot tea in front of me, along with a ham and cheese sandwich. I felt nauseated at the thought of eating, but Carrie said I needed to have food on my stomach for the pain pills, so I ate as instructed. She gave me some Tylenol and again asked me if I were sure she couldn't take me to the ER to be evaluated. I let her know that I would not go, no matter what. I thanked her anyway, especially for how they were doting over me.

"If I'm not gone before he comes back he will drag me right out of here and *make* me go back to that camper! He will *hurt* me again! I *have* to leave! I need to call my sister!" I shook uncontrollably. Carrie embraced me until I calmed down. I told them everything, spilling out all the bad that he made me feel, all the times he had physically assaulted me since I was first with him, and how he had begun to groom me at the age of fourteen to be an obedient woman. Carrie had already proven her friendship to me; I trusted her and didn't hold anything back.

I spilled out my fears of returning to that man. My stomach churned at the thought of it but my love for him confused me so badly. I knew the man was capable of severe abuse, yet I'd stayed with him. This time was the very worst and I didn't want to lose my life by giving him another chance.

Carrie brought me a canary-yellow phone, stretching the cord from the side wall. "Make any long-distance calls you need, Tammie, we will pay for them. And Tammie, we will pay to get you to San Antonio by bus, so you can fly out to wherever you need to go."

I called the only person I knew who was capable of paying for my ticket out and rescuing me. My sister Caroline and her husband Henry loved me so much. I always felt like Caroline was my second momma. I never called on her before, since I was convinced that Kevin had to teach me "valuable lessons," as he put it. She was so loving when I told her the basics of my story.

"Of course, I'm so sorry this all happened to you. Please tell Carrie and Liam we thank them so much! Are you going to be *okay* traveling? We'll take care of the flight arrangements, all you need to do is to get to the airport. Call me collect before you board the plane."

Carrie and Liam generously bought me a bus ticket for the 3-hour ride, as promised, and gave me money for a taxi to the airport. Also, some extra money for food for once I got to the airport. I'd fly to New Jersey, and stay with my family on the Naval Base until I figured things out.

I left without any further incident. Carrie and Liam had assured me that they would not call the police on Kevin, but that he would no longer be allowed to stay at their peaceful park.

A month later, I found myself working as a server at a local restaurant, saving my tips while living with my family in New Jersey. I was impressed by how big America was and that these people did not know what grits were! Being from the south everyone knew what grits were. I was trying to fit in as best I could, but I loved working and learning new things. When I wasn't at work I read novels every chance I could because their adventures took me to faraway places.

Sometimes while walking or conversing with others, out of nowhere I would flinch. An electric flash would cross my line of vision, mimicking Kevin's fist hitting me in the head. At a moment's notice, I was terror-stricken and paralyzed by the unmistakable trauma that was still very much alive inside me.

Once, while at work, I dropped an entire tray of food. Thank goodness it was in the back, at the kitchen area where the customers didn't see, but I knew everyone in the building could hear it. There were at least five plates of food on that tray! Luckily, I was able to cover it up with the explanation that I'd tripped!

I was trying desperately to make a new life for myself, but my nightmares returned. It was always the same. Kevin's abuse would find its way back into my life through torturous dreams of being chased by him. I just knew he was out there somewhere looking for me. I would wake up exhausted and sweaty. That's when I'd go to the kitchen for a glass of water and then go back to bed and sleep. That seemed to work for me.

As time passed, my thoughts of Kevin changed. I would find myself restlessly wondering what he was doing. Confusion between the beatings and the love I still had for him left me feeling empty, yet secretly yearning to just hear his voice again. I wondered if he ever thought of me, if he missed me, or was sorry that he hurt me.

At that time in my life, I wasn't thinking about how Kevin took criminal advantage of my age and vulnerabilities. No, he was all I knew of a man who had said he loved me, and I had thought that I loved him back.

Living with my sister and her family for those months allowed me to work and save some money. I loved roller skating with my niece, Stella Rae, on many cool afternoons there on the military base where we lived. She was six years younger than me, but I always thought she was the coolest kid I'd even known! I loved my Stella Rae. She was the sunshine on my dull days. When she walked into the room happiness followed her. My brother-in-law, Henry, renewed my pass that extended my stay on the base, but I knew I needed to figure out what I was going to do with my life.

One day after work, Caroline said that Momma had called for me and asked that I call her back. Momma had told Caroline that it was important and said that it had to do with Kevin.

I waited until after dinner to call her. I really wanted to know what he had said but I also had to consider why I would be discussing Kevin at all. Once the dishes were cleaned up, I phoned Momma. She said that Kevin's sister was trying desperately to contact me, that Kevin had been in a near-fatal accident.

CHAPTER ELEVEN

The Motorcycle Accident

1979 (17 Years Old)

As soon as I hung up the phone, I told Caroline and Henry that Momma had said that Kevin's sister, Peggy Sue, had called with terrible news. Kevin had been in an accident and was admitted to the Houston Medical Center, where he'd undergone extensive surgeries to his pelvis and leg areas. He was asking for me and Peggy Sue had requested that I call her.

Caroline asked, "are you going back to him, Tammie?"

"I don't know," I shrugged. "I don't think so. Well, maybe. I am always confused about what to do."

"Well, we are here for you, whatever you decide. You know that," Henry said.

I thanked them both and as I reached forward and gave my sister a big hug.

When I called Peggy Sue she told me, "I've been calling everywhere trying to locate you. Kevin feels bad for whatever happened between you two. He has been beating himself up over it, apparently for months. He's asking if you would please give him another chance, he says that he loves you very much!"

I got all the information from her and said that I'd be in touch. Peggy Sue and Kevin's brother, Daniel, were the only ones from his entire family that ever had an actual conversation with me. I felt horrible for Kevin. I missed him, and in some crazy way, I know I still loved him. I reflected if indeed there had been enough time and opportunity for him to come to his senses.

I took a couple of days to think about the situation. Then I called up Peggy Sue and told her that I was going. I gave notice at my job, with the hope that I would return soon. Three days after I first spoke with Peggy Sue, I said my good-byes to my family at the airport.

They wished me well, and told me to be careful and to call if I should ever need them. We hugged and I boarded my flight. I was Texas-bound once again, and hoping for a miracle.

The sight of him was painful to me! Seeing such a strong and healthy man bedridden and dependent was almost more than I could handle.

My heart had fallen to the floor, and I had to fight to keep the tears from spilling out. It was just so difficult for me to see him mangled up. The first thing he said was that he was sorry for what he'd done to me. He had worried himself sick over hurting me and asked for my forgiveness. He had had his sister keep calling around, looking for me until she found me.

Kevin was in the medical center for two months. Then his family drove us to their house on the east-coast of Florida, for another two months. After that he was ready to go back to his place out in Texas. Kevin's mother drove us back to Texas, for a follow-up with doctors and there we said good-bye to her. A friend of Kevin's, they called him Monkey, came to the medical center to drive us the last five and a half hours to Kevin's rental house. Back to the same town I had previously fled. It all seemed sur-real to me, but I tucked those feelings away. He was now wheelchair-bound, and in constant pain, but he was reluctant to take the pain medicine, for fear of developing an addiction.

It took a full year for him to recover and I was dedicated to taking care of him the entire time. I meticulously cleaned around each Steinman pin, twice a day, with sterile q-tips and Betadine. Then I applied antibiotic ointment and layers of gauze anchored with paper tape. I took much pride in my work. I cooked his meals, cleaned his house, and made stained glass pieces to sell.

It took Kevin a year to reteach his legs how to walk again. He would literally stand, leaning on crutches, while saying "leg move," and it wouldn't. Eventually, through those months of physical therapy, he began taking baby steps. He was on pain pills for over a year, though he took the least amount possible to make the pain tolerable. I thought it was quite remarkable to watch someone go from near death to a full recovery.

Though a lot had happened during that year, I always kept my distance from him, especially when he was mad at me. But I attributed his temper to his pain. Still, I had flashbacks of the physical and emotional pain he had caused me, and I continued to have intermittent sudden flashes of light that crossed my line of vision, from the past beatings I had received from him.

But there were also times when I reflected on how things must work out for a reason. It took that accident to bring me back to him. I did love him dearly. He told me that he loved me more than ever before and that he would never abuse me again and I was willing to trust him again. I truly believed that things would work out. I had been there for him and took care of him, during his most desperate times. That should count for something!

CHAPTER TWELVE

❖

Mazatlán, Mexico

1981 (18 Years Old)

Kevin was still recovering from the motorcycle accident when he first mentioned he wanted us to travel across Mexico to Mazatlán on the west coast. Going to the Baja Peninsula sounded like the other side of the world to me.

He had it all planned. He even had the map of Mexico with the route penciled in. We needed travel visas, which he told me we could get in Mexico. All he had to do was to pay them some money and they'd issue the visas on the Mexican side of the border.

A little under two years post-accident, he got the truck ready for the drive. He purchased new tires and extra parts for the engine, just in case, and stored them in the toolbox behind the driver's seat. New indoor/outdoor carpet had been installed in the back and he added a 1920s Progress Ice Box Fridge behind the passenger seat. The bed was an old feather mattress he had, with a blue-jean quilt his grandmother made. Kevin had taken the truck to a friend who created a secret compartment for the truck, welding it into the frame underneath the floor. It was only accessible under the carpet flap and only we knew it existed. He put all his money in that secret compartment and he had another one under the cushion of the driver's seat where he stashed his gun.

In March of 1981, we crossed the border into Ciudad, Acuna across from Del Rio, Texas. We got our visas, and took off driving into the interior of Mexico. I was eighteen years old.

It was the best day of my life. I began seeing the Mexican people, and started to understand how traditional were their lives. Once we left the narrow-paved road, it was all barren land with prickly pear cactus, sage bushes, and old dusty mesquite trees. There were thatched houses made of straw and donkeys and horses pulling carts with families on them. Only miles from the US border, the entire scenery had taken us to what seemed like another continent, far, far away!

The towns on our path were interesting and unique in their own ways. One thing though that remained the same in every town was the center city block. They were all beautiful, with concrete and tile sidewalks, a concrete bench or two, or three, or sometimes even more. It was the place where they celebrated their heritage. Many of the town centers had one or two statues or even a fountain (without water) and the occasional flag pole with the Mexican flag flying high. That simple central block was a place where the townspeople could come together and relax. Each city center was the resident's little oasis.

In the afternoons, as the sun beat with its brazen scorch, owners would close their shops for an hour or two. The locals would take to their favorite shady place for their siesta. Many moved mattresses out onto the ground under a tree, for their delicious naps.

Afterwards, the city would come alive again with the well-rested residents, fresh and ready for part two of their day. Mariachi bands played, standing proudly in their authentic dress, while their music echoed through the neighboring streets. Store owners flipped their signs and opened their doors, with business—as usual—resumed with smiles. Ice cream was sold from little stainless-steel carts on wheels. The aroma of roasted corn drifted through the air as it was skewered on a wooden stick, with a shake of cayenne pepper, and a squeeze of lime juice.

Our truck was old, so we didn't stick out that much, but when we were going slow through the towns, we were noticed more. People would stop and watch us pass. Children would start running along-side the truck, hoping for a glimpse or, if they were lucky, a treat of some kind.

The terrain remained flat and desert rough, for some time. Halfway across the country, outside the city of Torreón, we had to stop for a military road block. That was truly a scary experience. All the soldiers had on their uniforms with machine guns across their backs. Kevin got out and talked to them in Spanish. Meanwhile, ten or twelve solders surrounded the truck looking in the windows, and at me.

I tried to appear nonchalant. I didn't want them to see me watching them too! Kevin pulled out a stack of one-dollar bills and handed one out to every man, except to the ranking officer he gave three bills. They let us go and I had never been so relieved!

We only stopped at places to eat every other day just to have a warm homecooked meal. Otherwise, we ate canned food and fresh fruit and veggies that we picked up from markets along the way.

We stopped early one afternoon at an old roadside hotel for the night. All our clothes were dirty by then. We were tired from being on the road, and Kevin was in a lot of pain. The owner's wife had showed me where to do laundry. She took me to an open room with a normal sized bath tub. The ceramic floor of the tub was a wash-board. It was just like a tub is supposed to be, except this one was for sliding clothes over. It stood out to me because most washboards I'd used had been rougher, but the clothes came out so clean after I had scrubbed them. I then hung the clothes up inside our room to dry.

There was an attached restaurant at the hotel, but it was closed that day, because it was Sunday. We were out of groceries, and were craving a hot meal. Kevin talked the owners into opening the kitchen up that evening and cooking for us. Funny how anything warm with some flavor can seem like the best food you've ever tasted. That was the case that night.

Driving through the different towns along stretches of barren desert-lands, I saw so many little children with dried and bleeding lips from the sun. They would run up to the sides of the truck yelling different words, mostly ones I couldn't understand.

The Spanish seemed different throughout the interior than from the border. The difference in their Spanish was the accent, and they left no pauses between words. Their paragraphs seemed like one long word. Even though the accents changed, Kevin still seemed to understand and communicate well, which made our trip less complicated.

I had a few extra chap sticks at the time and I handed out what I had. The children were so grateful. One little boy shall linger in my memories forever. I gave a tube to him, and with a heavy tear about to spill over his lower eyelid, he quickly twisted off the cap and applied generous amounts and sighed. I vowed to never pass back through the interior again without boxes of lip balm to hand out to the children.

We crossed into the Sierra Madre Mountains and went to places where the people had never even seen an American girl before. One restaurant we stopped at for lunch was a small, old building about as long as a single car garage attached to a house. From the edge of the road, I looked at the building, awed that the restaurant didn't tumble down the mountainside from the cliff where it was anchored. The structure was held by stilted craftsmanship that formed a latticework along the cliff. We entered a small dining room that was lined with picnic tables and benches and sat down in a seat next to the window, where I looked down to see lush green tropical foliage and tree tops far in the distance below us.

As we sat there waiting for our breakfast, one by one, children began to enter and sit down a couple of tables away from us. They all sat lined up, facing us. Their elbows rested on the table and their little chins rested in their hands. There were about nine in all by the time the news got out to the whole neighborhood that we were there. They just sat there staring at us. Not giggling. Not whispering to each other. Just staring. I felt it was quite odd and it made me giggle, but Kevin explained to me that they were fascinated to see a blue-eyed American girl in their town, far in the depths of the Mexican mountains. He was right. It *was* me they were staring at!

I immediately loved every one of them, and found myself desperately wishing that I too lived there, in their lovely mountains. I gave them my brightest smile, straight from my heart, and as they smiled back I knew they'd received my love. I felt such a welcoming warmth from those people in the mountains, it was almost like coming home. I didn't understand how one could love a stranger, but I immediately loved those natives who lived high in the mountains, and missed them when we left.

We drove on roads around cliffs that appeared to only be big enough for one car but were actually frequented by eighteen-wheeler trucks! We watched for them, and were careful to stay away from them since they took up an entire curve. The cliffs at the curve were so steep, and the guardrails were only made of two by fours. They weren't exactly dependable. Before approaching a curve, we drove slowly and quietly, with windows open, to listen for a truck down shifting gears for his own approach to the curve. That was the only way we knew if a truck was coming!

We even drove across water once, where a river flooded the road. We waited until another car showed up and crossed with no problem. We wanted to be careful since we were not from there and didn't know if this was normal, or a flood! It was scary enough when we braved it, but we made it across safely.

We spent days traveling through the winding hillsides, avoiding herds of sheep being guided by their herders on the sides of the road, and the mist that made it difficult to see at times. We stopped many times, just to take in the quiet landscape that seemed so tranquil and magically unreal to our minds. We saw strange birds of exotic colors and tropical plants growing out of the sides of the mountain while water streamed over the rocky ledges. There were lush trees with big white flowers hanging facedown, resembling large bells. Some areas were covered with clover that spilled over into the streams, speckled with an array of floral delight. There were numerous narrowed bridges that were only wide enough for one car. I took it all in with a deep breath, closed my eyes and thought, *what a beautiful journey through a country that not a lot of people from my homeland have seen.*

When we had passed the last deserted section of the mountain range, the road opened up to the city of Mazatlán on the coast. The breeze was coming into the truck windows with a hint of salt in the air. Our trip across Mexico had taken us about two weeks, since Kevin was unable to sit in the vehicle for long periods of time.

The trip wasn't without complications. Kevin was frequently angry and mean to me. I was afraid of him falling back into the same old abusive Kevin, so I just separated myself from his nasty language and his anger that seemed to escalate whenever we had driven non-stop for hours on end. He always made it clear to me that I had made him angry, and that I needed to keep my mouth shut and listen to him. That is what he said to me every time he had back-handed me while on the road. I separated those incidents from my mind, attributing them to his pain from the accident.

In Mazatlán, the streets were busy as we used a map to find the downtown area, our destination. Finally pulling down several city blocks, turning right and left, Kevin pulled into the parking lot of a hotel. There was the familiar odor of sewage that was present in many towns across Mexico. The hotel room was white concrete all around, the floor, ceiling, and walls. There was a deep concrete seat at the base of the window with burglar bars. The warm spring breeze was constant and mixed with the cool sea breeze, creating the perfect conditions for a nap.

This was night one, in our destination city on the western coast of Mexico. Within a couple of days, we found an apartment to rent. We paid for one month.

I sat one morning, a week later, writing in my journal about the trip so far.

Journal Entry
March 17, 1981

"[Kevin] and I have been having such a joyous time off the coast of the Baja of California, in Mazatlán, Mexico. Perhaps he is finally feeling better and more recovered from the accident now. I hope so, he's gone through a lot of pain.

He's been being nice to me, he's not even reading my daily logs anymore, not that I say anything wrong in them!

I have thought about my family a lot since we have been here, because my family lives near the beach too, I want to think that they are just up the road, but Florida's east coast is a world away. [Kevin] says it costs too much to call them from Mexico, that I'll have to wait until we get back to Texas.

We have spent a great deal of our time swimming in the pacific oceans. We rented surf boards today, and I surfed for the first time in my life! That was so much fun! Then we paddled on those same surf boards across the open ocean to the island offshore. There we petted the miniature donkeys, had lunch, and swam in the water.

While at that island today I was stung by a jellyfish! I suddenly felt a sting and turned around to see where it was coming from, there was nothing there. As I kept turning around in circles looking for it, the jellyfish's long tentacles kept wrapping around me. [Kevin] pulled me from the water, as I was kind of yelling and making my pain known to everyone. A couple of people ran over to help, they told me roll in the sand to get a layer formed. Then one guy took a shell and started scrapping at my back in several places until he pulled away tentacles, by grabbing it between two shells. He told me to stand up as he pulled them from all the way around me.

Then they smooth rubbed the sand over my red
streaks, to make sure there weren't anymore. I got
back in the water to rinse off the sand. Someone
brought over vinegar, for us to apply. It was an
awful experience. It burned to the core! It was
worse than a sunburn! I had to re-apply the sun-
screen, and we decided to take the ferryboat back
to the mainland today with boards in tow."

Kevin seemed to be in his element. He always said things like
"You can't cheat an honest man." While traveling or lounging at the
beach he was always teaching me his knowledge of logic. "You trust
only me. Everyone is out to steal your freedom! No one will ever care
about you the way I do. I know your heart. No one else will ever have
your best interest in mind. Everyone will always be out to use you, no
matter how sincere they may seem! The world is a rotten, evil place.
The government is even worse."

Journal Entry
March 20, 1981

"This morning I slept in but woke up immediately to a screaming female, which was easy, since
the French doors to the balcony were both left
wide opened. The voice sounded like that of a
young woman in her early 20s, not much older
than me! I wrapped the sheet around me and ran
to the balcony to see, the young woman was airborne! She was nearly approaching the road in
front of the apartment building, coming from
the beach. "Parasailing."
    Apparently, the boat had stalled. Between
the winds and the current of the waves, it had
shoved the boat ashore keeping the woman high
in the sky. She was not only hovering over land
but near my street, even worse getting close to the

power lines! I threw on some clothes, grabbed my keys, and slid my feet into my flip flops. I don't know where [Kevin] was at this point! I quickly ran down the concrete stairs, and then across the road. By this time I'm yelling to her that I will get help. She yelled back to me, 'Please hurry!!'

Back at the shoreline, the captain of the small ski boat, was frantically gathering people by yelling for help to get his customer back to land! He had three people helping when I showed up, then there were six, then nine, then fifteen. We were pulling the rope with all our might, it just wasn't moving her very fast! That poor young woman, we could hear her high pitch scream as she got closer to live wires. More people kept showing up. Until we must've had some twenty-plus people yanking the rope with desperation to get this woman out of harm's way!! Together we pulled and retrieved her just in time to save her from danger! She was shaken up to say the least! There were so many vacationers looking on, standing on the beach, cheering on as she landed her feet to the sand. We had hands on every inch of that rope! There was still a lot of cheering and yelling as she was being released from her harness. She said that she will never do that again!

It was just another great day in Mazatlán!"

There was such a mix of different cultures living in our apartment complex including French, Spanish, Asian, and Italian. We had an interesting life among those people since they were usually drunk. Kevin let me drink sometimes, but only one at a time. He didn't want me to engage in a conversation with any of them. He let me sit and listen, as long as he was with me. One afternoon in the courtyard as we were all sitting around the terrace, he told the group of foreigners that I couldn't hear very well, and that it was best not to speak to me. I silently grimaced at that statement, because it just sounded so abrupt and wasn't part of what they were talking about at all.

One of them, who I knew had heard what Kevin said, responded in a rather strong French accent with "I'm sorry, what did you say? I didn't hear you. It's because I'm hard of hearing, ya know?" They were beginning to make fun of 'the old guy Kevin.' They were all closer to my age than Kevin's.

Kevin snapped back, "She's pretty to look at but don't speak to her!"

They all busted out laughing, speaking in their native tongue to each other, which really made Kevin mad. He stiffened up in his posture, but he chuckled along for a few minutes, to save his own pride. Then he was done with them, I could tell, so we headed back to the apartment. He was fine when it was just us. When someone else came in to the picture, the old Kevin came out just enough to make my stomach churn sour.

Besides Kevin's unscrupulous knack for jealousy, and only the occasional incident of back-handing me for not listening, it was nice living there.

Journal Entry
March 23, 1981

"We wake up every day with coffee and breakfast on our minds. I always hurry to shower and dress for the day, so he doesn't have to wait on me. He isn't happy when I get in his way. [Kevin] says it's the woman's job to be disciplined and put her man first in every thought.

Today we went to the beachfront café on the main boulevard and had Huevos Rancheros! It was SO good! We ordered orange juice and watched from our table as the guy fed the fresh halved oranges onto the squeezer. He lowered the handle and pushed down onto the orange, out came the orange juice! Then we ate our breakfast and enjoyed our freshly squeezed orange juice. All the while watching a rather oversized lizard about 2+ feet long. It was moving steadily, in an almost slow-motion fashion, across the overhang of the terracotta roofing. The waiter said that was "Jose" and that he was their pet iguana.

✦

We're now at the beach and I'm writing while lying on a chair provided by the restaurant, where we just ate a late lunch. I'm watching this Mexican guy with a tray of rings and bracelets, go from person to person calling out, "five-dollar rings!" He just left us. [Kevin] bought me a silver ring with an oval-shaped black onyx, and a silver bracelet with a giant mother of pearl butterfly. I am wearing it right now, it's so pretty.

Well, [Kevin] is so quiet today, we are both trying to get used to the fact that it's time to go back to the states soon."

We stayed there for a month, then returned to Texas. Six months later we went back to Mazatlán. The landlady had already reserved our apartment for our return date. It was an American woman who rented the apartment to us. She lived somewhere down the road in a fancy high rise. Once, I rode with Kevin there and had to stay in the cab for thirty minutes while he went up to see her. We were able to afford our apartment since Kevin put thirty thousand American dollars in the Mexican bank, we lived off the interest. Kevin had settled from his motorcycle accident and that was what was left. At least that's what Kevin said. He never once gave me money. He said that money was to be carried by the man, not the woman.

The journeys across the interior of Mexico, to the Pacific coastline and back to Texas were beyond my imagination. I was in awe of the culture and divine landscapes as we drove Kevin's Dodge panel truck through valleys, across water, through narrowed pathways, and around mountains' ledges. Beauty lay around every curve and within every local native. Kevin unfolded this life of beauty to me. He showed love to my fragile heart and made me believe in him again. My love for him, once again, grew stronger every day that we were away. His master plan with full control over me, once again, was established.

CHAPTER THIRTEEN

Isolation

1983 (21 Years Old)

Stand By Me

Come, stand by me,
As you look at what I see,
Rescue me from these raging seas,
Please come stand by me to set me free!

We had driven to Florida on one of our yearly trips home. As the years folded past, Kevin steadily began changing into a different person. It was especially bad when we arrived at his family's house. He became increasingly more abusive to me. He wouldn't let me hang around him. It was almost as though he had to prove to his family that I meant nothing to him. The only reason I ever wanted to go to Florida was, so I could go and see my own family, though my visit was always limited to forty-five minutes. One visit. One time. He would always make me wait until we were at his family's house and he was in the mood before he would give permission for me to phone Momma. This was only if I didn't bug him about it. Momma always had the job of contacting relatives to tell them that I was home and that I would be there the following morning. Of course, not all family members were able to be there at such short notice. I had an hour total, from the time I left Kevin's side.

Two years had passed since our last trip down to the coast of Mexico. Kevin had moved us all over the place living out of his camper. He was growing restless. He was always in pain, at least that's what he said, but he didn't believe in pain pills. He certainly didn't believe in ever going back to the doctors either. He only went before when he had no choice because of the accident. And the follow-ups recommended by his attorney, in getting the settlement he wanted. The violence worsened. If I made him mad, it didn't matter who was there, I was sure to get backhanded in the face. Afterwards it was always the same. He'd love on me, which would disgust me. I did love him, or at least I thought I did. I was massively confused about what love even meant. He told me to learn to be good and not to piss him off. I supposed it was a concept I just wasn't getting!

Slowly my life began changing with him. He had moved us out to the barren desert with the plan to build a house without any electricity or running water. He encouraged me to work a lot, giving me strict instructions about what to do. He told me it would pay off when it was time to see my family. I never asked what that meant; it only made me excited to think of seeing them! He had left me a lot recently in the camper out in that desert, all by myself. It scared me so badly! He had said that he had just needed to take care of a few things. Each time was for several days.

This time, when we went to Florida, I was anxious and really missed my family. I wanted them to believe that I was succeeding in my life with Kevin. I didn't want them to think I had failed, as Kevin had said so many times that I would if I left him. I didn't want my parents to be worried for me, or sad that they'd made the wrong decisions by letting me go, so I never told them about the abuse I suffered. He had me convinced that I was solely dependent on him to have any chance in this world. Failing was such a big word and it terrified me into submission. His mantras to me were always, "my way or the highway," or "if you leave me you'll fail, and you will never be allowed back," or "you're nothing without me." I always believed him. He had years to brainwash me. He stripped me of my courage and self-image.

The day I arrived at my parent's house on that particular trip, we all hugged and shared greetings and then everyone sat and stared at each other. I was taking in their facial features and their voices, trying to gather an album of memories to take when I left. We knew this would be all we would get, that I would not be returning tomorrow nor next week, as I always said I would, and never did. I wasn't able to answer all the many questions they had, like, "Tammie why do you stay with him? I can see you're not happy," "why do you not just tell him that you want more time with us? Don't you want to be around us?" or, "what makes you so afraid of him? Does he hurt you?"

I laughed off their questions like they were ridiculous. "Of course I'm happy!" and, "we have plans, but if I have time I'll come back, I promise!" "Afraid? Naw! Don't say such crazy things. I love Kevin! He would never hurt me!"

They knew me. They were staring me square in the eyes, especially my childhood bestie cousins. I desperately wanted them to believe that I was okay, so they didn't spend the next year worrying over me. The part of me that thought I loved him didn't want to speak badly of him. And I couldn't leave him and take the chance that he'd be right and that I'd fail without him. That would be huge to me, the subservient, dependent woman I'd grown into!

I got to hear updates on who had babies, who got married, who graduated high school, and even who was in college now. I also took five minutes to grieve with Momma about the recent death of her mom, my grandma, who I loved dearly. "She didn't suffer, it happened while she was in surgery."

They all talked about good times. It wasn't difficult to see deeper than the smiles, the worry that they felt for me. Their concern lingered in my thoughts long after I left their side.

My cousins and I were all twenty-one that year. They were so excited about the new dance club, Levi Palace. On the grand opening, the township had managed to book David Frizzell and Shelly West! I was ecstatic!

One of my very favorite songs was "You're the Reason God Made Oklahoma." I had heard that song on the radio out in Texas while riding with Kevin to a nearby town. "Going to another town" out in Texas usually meant at least a couple-hour ride, no matter which direction you went. That was the highlight of those days, being asked to ride with him, instead of him leaving me behind. He would always take me to a Dairy Queen for ice cream and I would think, *ah, the luxuries of life!*

Excitement and conversation made my visit pass quickly. I lost track of the time and had to say goodbye in a hurry, as I gave hugs all around and quickly left. But I didn't leave without taking time for one last glimpse of my loving family, who all stood in the yard waving good-bye.

But time was short, so I drove away, back to Kevin's parents' house while I thought about how I was missing out on everyone's lives. They seemed to miss me terribly, and that somehow brought comfort to my broken soul. I couldn't quite understand why I didn't have more self-control to leave him, or even just share my wants with him. As my family said, "why don't you just ask him, Tammie?"

Arriving at his family's house, I could see that they were waiting for me so we could go to the market. I looked at the clock on the dash. "Oh my goodness!" I was fifteen minutes late! After I parked his truck, I jumped into the back seat of his mother's Buick. Kevin was sitting next to his mother, Sue Ellen, who was driving.

I knew that my family would be going to Levi Palace tonight to see the concert and I wanted nothing more in the whole world than to join them. They'd given me so much confidence with their love that I began telling Kevin all about it, enthusiastically. Really, they all thought it was a bit strange that I didn't have more freedom, and I told Kevin a little about that too. All I wanted was an excuse to see them all again! I told him that I loved them all, and missed my bestie cousins! They all wanted to see more of me, so "could I please go back and just spend the day with my family?"

"Why are you telling me about these people and where they're going tonight? It has nothing to do with you!" Kevin exclaimed.

I remembered this moment with great clarity for a long time afterwards. "I just thought it would be nice to see more of my family. Kevin, I really do miss them!" I cried earnestly. "It's amazing, my little brother is so much bigger now! And the concert sounded like it'd be so much fun! You promised me that you wouldn't keep me away from them...."

I was so caught up in what I was saying, that his blow was unexpected. He reached into the back seat with a fist and made contact with my face. His anger escalated with loud breaths and tightened lips.

I cried inside myself, *how could I not have realized that this would happen? I should've been more careful!*

"Your parents gave you to me! I will not allow you to *hang out* with them! Have I not said this enough, or are you just too plain *stupid* to hear me? You will *listen* to me and you *will* do things MY way, am I understood! I am the one who puts food in your stomach, I am the one who puts up with your whining! I was also the one who took you in when your 'family' no longer wanted anything to do with you! So, sit your little ass right there, and keep that mouth of yours shut, do you hear me? I don't want to hear another word about that family of yours! And you have just lost next year's privilege to see those people, I will not have them corrupting your mind again!"

The mother said quietly, "you really shouldn't do that, It's just not good for the girl."

Contemptuously, he replied, "I love you, but you need to mind your own business, woman."

She concluded with "...just saying..."

And that was that.

Our trip to Florida was for a total of six weeks. Kevin told me how he had planned on spending "some quality time," with his parents, grandparents, sisters, brothers, cousins, and his close friends.

My parents still only lived a couple of miles down the road.

He made me stay in the living room while the "adults" watched TV and hung out in the den. One thing I could never shake, no matter how hard I tried, was that sick feeling deep inside. I felt the solitude and the shame of not fitting in, sitting there like a dog waiting to be spoken to, it all stirred deep inside my stomach. The only way to avoid the thick acidic coating from consuming my youth, was to go to sleep. I had that feeling most of the time we were in Florida, around his family.

I could hear the television in the background in the den, where Kevin and his family were. The space shuttle was being launched from Cape Canaveral. My family always loved watching the shuttle pass over the Florida skies. I wondered if my presence still lingered in their minds. I liked to think that they loved me, as they said they did, and perhaps mourned my absence, as I mourned theirs.

I felt worthless. How could I be so shallow as to think working extra-long hours back in Texas would bring even one humane moment to this man's heart? He could be so soothing with his words at times, and then suddenly turn callous. Those words and the humiliation of being hit in front of his family always silenced me and left me feeling lonely, dirty, and unwanted. I had to close my eyes and go to that place of calm. I wanted to feel sorry for myself, but I feared if I did, it would surely engulf me and turn me into something I didn't want to become.

I spent the rest of the week sleeping as much as I could. I couldn't allow the razor edge words to cause me anymore pain. I tried to forget that image of a mad man whose eyes bore through me with such hate and contempt.

He told his family that it was up to him to protect me from mine, that they would only corrupt my mind, and that I belonged to him. Because he'd put all that work into me, I would never be allowed more than forty-five minutes a year with "those people." He simply couldn't imagine why I'd want to be around them.

I imagined that his family thought no more about me and the abuse I endured in their presence. His family never accepted me. They were discouraged from speaking to me. They never invited me to look at pictures or spoke to me about the weather, cooking, or politics. Nothing. Neither parent had ever even made eye contact with me. I was as alone there in my hometown, as I was in the desert.

There would never be someone to come and rescue me from that abusive situation. It was my life. When I visited my family, I was an actor who always strove to leave on a positive note—a happy performance. It's just who I had become.

The humility and treatment I received was unbearable at times. It was especially difficult knowing that my family could easily tell that I was still in town. On some visits, we were in town for another two months after my one forty-five-minute visit to my parents' home. Kevin's truck could be seen in the driveway of his parents' business where we stayed, by anyone driving by.

I often sat in the stillness of the darkened front living room, at his parent's house, looking out through the tinted front window, at highway 49, at the cars as they passed. I angrily thought to myself, *I don't even know how to identify my own family's cars.* I wasn't allowed to be around them long enough to even know what they drove!

How could it be that I would turn into a statistic? "She was a troubled kid," "a bad girl!" and "we had no control over her," were all I remembered of what people said of me. They never said "Tammie. She is such a loving person with a heart of gold." I silently assessed myself. *Kevin certainly has no difficulty in controlling me.*

I couldn't help but feel let down by my entire community. There were those who should've fought to the bitter end for me, but they did nothing. Especially the ones related to Kevin, who witnessed the abuse themselves.

He didn't hit me as much in front of his parents as he did in the privacy of his bedroom at their house. I tried my best not to get him mad. It was difficult to take back what I said to him.

He would snatch my forearm and squeeze tightly, saying, "I do not like being disrespected!" It was senseless to try and rationalize with him once he got started, I had never succeeded in defusing his temper. Not once. The memory of his punches and open-handed swats played over in my mind, repeatedly. Sometimes I would forget entire days that had been spent in contemplating his abuse. I would cry out for him to stop, but he was obsessed. He believed that I had stepped over his imaginary line again! He would shove me into that room and close the door in a rage. He would get me in the corner, smashing his hand hard over my mouth. He would push himself onto me against my wishes. I did what I learned as a child, mentally leaving my body just so I could cope. I would separate my mind from that version of Kevin.

I just couldn't understand how I could make him *that* angry. I tried to not be a broken person, but it tore my spirits down. Having no conversations with anyone left me isolated. Kevin's brother, Daniel, did talk with me a little when he was around. He mostly stayed away when we were in Florida, saying that he couldn't handle the way Kevin spoke to me, and that this was best. His brother had told me many times, that he would kill Kevin if he ever laid a hand on me.

He was the only one who didn't know the true extent of the abuse I endured at Kevin's hands. I always believed his brother, that he would've hurt Kevin if he had known about the physical part. I just couldn't let that happen.

I never told on Kevin to anyone. Most of his family knew that I was deprived of basic human rights, and most of them had seen me being physically abused.

They too are in on the abuse, I thought. *The verbal, emotional, and physical abuse. They all see and hear it happening.*

He beat me. And frequently. I didn't understand why he believed that I deserved such treatment. Somehow, I knew, deep in my heart, that the day would come when I would break free. I would never return to him again, nor to the family who never rescued me from his wrath.

As months turned into years, I constantly prayed that God would preserve me. I grew into a woman, but never into an adult. I stayed the young girl Kevin wanted me to be.

He used me. I was his puppet. When he said sit, I sat. When he said stand, I stood.

He had clearly convinced himself and his family that I had no family of my own. "They don't deserve to see you more than the allotted time I have given. That was the agreement!" he would say. So, in my life of solitude, I slept for most of our Florida trips. I wanted someone to rescue me, but knowing they wouldn't, I saw no reason to stay awake.

CHAPTER FOURTEEN

Grace Never Ending

1986 (24 Years Old)

Back to my hometown where I had grown up, Kevin kept me close to him all the time. I was forbidden to touch the phone! I was only allowed to leave the property with him. I couldn't even go to the store with his mother. He told me that his Mom wasn't responsible enough to watch over me. Only he had an eagle's eye and that no one else could be trusted with his precious gem. No one was going to put a damper on his party.

No amount of experience with Kevin could ever have prepared me for the change in his personality once we were around his daughter. She was home from college, and her mother, Monica was dropping her off to visit for the day. Kevin's changed attitude toward me during their visit illustrated the low status I held in that man's heart. As though I needed more clarification!

Around his family, it was true, I never knew how to act. After all, he had never declared to them who I was. Was I his girlfriend, his wife, his friend, or his servant? Every single trip he repeated the same story to anyone who wanted to listen. He said that it had all been "very legal," and that I was "given" to him by my parents. I was always in earshot of all those lies. All I wanted to do was to cover my face. Those words brought me shame and embarrassment. I made a

mental note, many times, that if I survived this life of mine, the stories would not go untold! "Someday," I thought, "they will all know
the truth!"

Our annual visit to Florida began as it always did. The ritual
visit to my family passed uneventfully, and it was time for his visitors
from North Carolina. I was told that Monica had been Miss North
Carolina at one time, and that she was still a true beauty.

Tonya was the older of Kevin's two daughters and she was very
polite when first introduced. But as soon as her beauty queen mother
left, Kevin started barking orders at me, treating me vulgarly. It was
as though he wanted to display to his daughter that I was nothing
more than a servant. I was only eight years older than her.

I was stunned. I was still in the mindset that he really loved
me. He ordered me to unload Tonya's pillow cases of dirty clothes,
although Tonya attempted to object. He told her just to watch at
how he had trained me to do things like that. As I looked at him I
saw him more clearly than ever before. He was gloating over his prize!
I inwardly declared that I was not slave material! I was a real catch,
and Kevin knew that, so he had to keep me humiliated and feeling
worthless just to keep me at all!

I caught a glimpse of his face and thought, *my family would feed
you to the alligators if they knew how you're treating me!*

Tonya didn't seem too interested in his games. I truly believe
that she was prepped by her mother beforehand. She just wanted to
leave and go shopping with Kevin's mother, Sue Ellen, as planned.
Sue Ellen had never asked for me to go places with her.

As his family left, I was in the washhouse sorting out the laundry. I carefully followed the instructions on each item, as Tonya was
a college student, and dressed very preppy (not that I had even a clue
what preppy was). I only knew that the clothes were interesting to
look at. I tried to imagine what they would look like on me, since
Tonya and I were the same size. I had already washed most of the
clothes, except for one load that was just finishing the spin cycle,
when Kevin announced that we would be leaving in a few minutes to
go stay at his grandparents' house. "Deal with it," he barked. "Take

them wet!" He told me that I could hang them out at his grandparents' house when we arrived in an hour.

I never got used to the feeling of my face going pale white. My personality was not a shy one, but Kevin had changed everything about me. I was constantly embarrassed and fearful. I knew that at any moment I could say the wrong thing, or do something wrong or not fast enough and he would lose patience and fly into a rage.

As we headed to Kevin's grandparents' house, I was carried, once again, far from my childhood home and family.

Kevin's mother arrived soon after we did and dropped off Tonya before leaving.

I carried the clothes through the living room on my way to the back door to hang them out on the line to dry. As I passed Kevin, who was already sitting in a recliner with iced tea in hand and feet up, he snatched my arm tightly, causing me to drop everything. "When you're finished with that, I want you to ask if my daughter wants something to eat or drink. You are to keep her happy while she's here, am I understood?"

Kevin was at least *sometimes* nice to me back in Texas. But he was always unpredictable. I surely felt abused enough as it was, I felt my face go pale once again. His family was there, watching and listening. He then said, with an even sterner tone that sent those familiar shivers up and down my spine, "are you listening to me, or do I need to slap some sense into that *stupid* head of yours?"

I snapped out of it and told him that I understood. I picked up the clothes while everyone watched.

I had hung the clothes on the lines outside and waited patiently for them to dry. Outside. I never went back inside to wait on Tonya, hoping that Kevin's grandmother had taken on that job. I neatly folded and packed the clothes back in the pillowcases, as instructed, and proudly presented the bundles, perhaps looking for some shred of humanity. With condescension dripping from his tongue, and again in front of his family, he ordered that I go sit in the back room while he visited with his daughter and her mother.

I left the eyes that followed me out of sight. I went to the same room, as always, with the picture windows and starched sheets. I sank on to the bed and pulled out a book. I loved reading, since it helped me escape from my own reality. Danielle Steele novels took me away to the faraway lands of California. The stories I read were always about a strong-willed female, mostly from a royal bloodline. Some stories were of a young woman running away from her wealthy family to find a life on her own, living in a flat and working for some publishing company. There was always a man of her dreams that would sweep her off her feet, and take her to live in some big gothic mansion, usually with horses and a pool that she did laps in every day of her life. I read until I fell asleep.

I began dreaming of my family, from when I was a young girl. In my dream, I would wake up and run to the kitchen where I would see all the faces of my loved ones sitting around the kitchen table, having coffee, and laughing. They would be just the way I left them so many years before. I remembered their loud boisterous laughs, but my grandmother's clucking laughter would stand out most in my memory. I loved being surrounded by that happiness shared by my momma's family. It had been there my entire childhood. In my dreams, they would all be together at the dining room table, laughing and playing Parcheesi, Grandpa's favorite game.

When Kevin came in to wake me up, the delicious afternoon nap had left me in a stupor. The filtered daylight reflected the afternoon sun preparing to set in the evening sky. He sat on the side of the bed, caressing my hair. He said that Tonya and her mother had left for their home in North Carolina. In an almost gentle whisper he told me that I had done a "really good job" taking care of his daughter and that he was very proud of how well I listened. There it was! That little bit of love that was just enough to make me light-headed and falling back in love with his gentleness. He told me that we would be going back to his parent's house for the night since there was church meeting in his grandparents' house the next morning and he didn't want to sleep there that night.

I hated staying at his parent's house. Kevin and I didn't even sleep together there, which felt a bit ironic since we did at his grandparents' house. It just seemed oddly backwards to me. I had to sleep on a couch in the living room at the center of the house, surrounded by the people who were so cold to me. I was sharply instructed to "stop complaining!" about where I was sleeping whenever I mentioned it. Kevin said I was lucky to have a couch! I didn't ask what that meant. I could hear his mother in the kitchen, as always, using the Lord's name in vain over and over, like she could think of no other words to use. I thought to myself, *wasn't anyone around those people when they were young, who told them that they weren't supposed to do that?*

It wasn't long before we left for our long and dismal drive back to Texas. I always despised the drive back to the solitude of that dry-cracked hill. Though the weather was hot, it was still technically early springtime, so the temperatures wouldn't be quite so ridiculous. Kevin had already gone down the *to do* list for our arrival back. Unlike myself, he was anxious to get back to work on the house.

I yearned for acceptance on so many levels, and I was terrified of retribution if I did not do as I was told. Humiliation was a way of life. I was taught from an early age that women are vulnerable to men. My own physical and emotional strength may not have stopped him from keeping me broken and fearful, but there was a presence that protected me from becoming totally shattered. I always sensed the presence of God, so I knew I was not forgotten. God helped me resist the trauma that I experienced.

I was not alone.

I was never ever alone.

CHAPTER FIFTEEN

—◆—◆—

The Rio Grande

1986 (24 Years Old)

During my earlier years in Texas, life was sometimes amazing. When Kevin was not being mean to me, there was a glimmer of hope that perhaps I'd become the woman he always wanted me to be. We lived on a tall hill that overlooked an onion and cantaloupe farm of about two-thousand acres. The farm was on US soil. To the south of the farmland, barely distinguishable to the naked eye, was a line of trees. Those trees lined the riverbank of the Rio Grande, which served as the International Border Line between Texas and Mexico.

My favorite place on the property was in the front yard. I took pride in arranging new rocks in my garden that we'd bring back from the river or from a walk on his twenty acres of land, that was about three miles on the other side of town. I did a lot of things on the front porch, where I was safe from the snakes, scorpions, and other crawlers that lived in the desert. I watched the sunsets, I spoke to the moon, and I searched the night sky for shooting stars. I watched the silent sunrises, and drank my morning tea there too, unless the flies were already swarming.

From that porch, I often stood and watched for the dust trail, across the valley in the distance, stirred up by farm trucks. That's when Kevin would let me drive by myself. I'd take the truck to the bottom of the hill, and gather the onions or cantaloupe that would fall unscathed into the sage brush. The big farm trucks would sway from side to side as they climbed up and onto the paved road. The top of the heap would go flying everywhere! I remember how giant yellow onions and cantaloupe would crash onto the road and split open. The strong sweet smell settled across the valley during the harvest time of the season. That was so much a part of my environment. I loved eating the ripened cantaloupe and, though I didn't like onions much, it made me feel good to pick them and bring them back up to the house.

Kevin would occasionally take me to the river banks north of the town in which we lived. He said that it was a five-hour trip by car to the next town to the north, so the river flowed untainted for hundreds of miles through the desert wilderness. He also said that it would be cleaner than the south side of town because it flowed from north to south.

He would pull off the main road and drive his old truck down a dirt road as far as he could. We would walk the rest of the way. He always packed his gun wherever we went. He taught me sternly that the way people die is when they can't protect themselves.

I spent many hours lying on the refreshing river rocks of the Rio Grande. The rocks were smooth, and not jagged. Many people believed that the entire run of the Rio Grande is dirty water. But I spent many years in the waters north of town, and it was clear and only a foot or two deep. It had an earthy scent. During the hot days (and every day was hot) it was pure heaven!

The area we always went to was desolate, with no people for miles in any direction. In certain areas of the Rio Grande, beneath the brush on the riverbanks, was mud, but not the gritty kind of mud one normally finds. The mud of the Rio Grande is the smoothest, creamiest charcoal black mud. I wore a bikini to have more exposed skin surface. I would smooth handfuls of mud all over my exposed skin, layers upon layers. Then, with the full-shade of the Cinzano umbrella in hand, I'd sit on the rocks just above the waters reach. Before long, the warm wind and heat would dry the mud and, piece by piece, it would fall off in chunks.

There is no other place on earth that could match the tranquility of that land.

Sometimes he took me to his twenty acres of land. He always said that we'd build a house there too. It was all deserted desert land. We would drive the old truck off the road into the desert until there was no one for miles.

I'd wear a thin cotton dress, or shorts with a long-sleeved chambray shirt and a wide-brimmed sombrero on my head. And boots! I always wore boots in the desert. We each brought a canteen of water strapped over a shoulder. Sometimes Kevin brought beer, though very rarely did he let me drink.

We walked for miles and miles. It was the most beautiful thing I ever did. Walking in total silence except for the wind when it swept across the canyons. We lowered ourselves to the arroyos where rivers had once flowed. Never once did we ever see another human being on our walks. As I recall, there were no demarcations plotting off the back side of his property, just the markers close to the road. I grew to love that dry, cracked earth.

There were good moments in Texas, but I knew this was only because of my relationship with nature. No matter how long I lived on this earth, I knew that I desperately wanted to remember my desert experience!

I was never threatened, nor approached by any illegal immigrants. They would frequent the property late in the night on their journey in search of their "American Dream."

I had a tender giving heart. It was a fact that the Mexicans were hungry and thirsty by the time they walked across that hill, where I lived. There were many times that I would leave tortillas and gallon jugs of water for them. Sometimes I could hear them outside. They never once tried to break in, but I was prepared to shoot them, if they had.

Mostly they were hardworking Mexican men, searching for work so they could send money back to their poor families. They were simple people desiring more than the dirt-poor lifestyle they were accustomed to. They never traveled alone, but watched each other's backs and worried for their brothers. They'd come from far away, from the interior of Mexico, and even from further south than Mexico, walking through miles and miles of scorching searing heat. That intense heat would beat down on their hats and rise from beneath their shoes. They carried tortillas, beans, and a small supply of water for their long trips. If they were lucky enough to not be killed by an animal or person, die of dehydration, or get deathly sick drinking from a contaminated water source, they'd finally make it to the farmlands across from where I lived.

Once they arrived at the border, these people were utterly exhausted and starving! They were at risk of being trafficked to work at other places across the states and there were many other dangers too. I'd heard that sometimes they died in the trucks that delivered them to their jobs. I couldn't imagine surviving such a tremendous journey, only to die in the US, inside a moving vehicle. It made me sad to hear about it. Kevin told me some stories, but he didn't tell me as many as I figured he must know.

That's why I always took that small pleasure in giving needed water and bread.

Water was a commodity for even us, on that hill. It had to be hauled to the property in large blue barrels. We'd never had running water though I'd done all I could to get water to his property, but to no avail! For months, every night and into the early morning hours Kevin would lower me into that hole that was going to be the well. He had constructed a windlass over the well, strong enough to support his own weight. As I dug deeper, he built a wooden casing which supported only the first twenty-five feet of the well wall. For the next twenty-five feet, I had to be careful not to touch the sides while being lowered, so as not to disturb the rocks on the walls. When Kevin cranked the bucket up to the top, full of rocks, he had to go slow to avoid touching the walls. I didn't even have a hard hat to protect me. I used a pick ax to dislodge the tightly formed rocks, gravel and limestone clay. Caliche ground was technically underground sediment cement, bonded with calcium carbonate and other minerals to form rock, making most of it too hard for even hand drills to penetrate. This was why there were vast amounts of vacant desert lands across Texas. That and the water table is far underground.

Kevin would lower the bucket, sometimes only able to raise one large rock at a time. He had to be the first person to go down in the well every day since I refused to go down until all the scorpions were killed. Any time during the day or night it wasn't unusual for the border patrol helicopter to fly over the well area, checking for wetbacks. They'd shine a high-powered spotlight into the deep hole, and always see the same American girl, deep inside the pit. Usually cheap, illegal labor dug wells by hand. The only difference was that I received no payment as a hired hand. I was free for anything Kevin needed me for.

Out in that west Texas town where I grew up, I had become the desert's daughter. My love grew deep in the roots of that desert terrain. I loved the feeling of being in the presence of those natural elements of the Rio Grande. For me, the hard work had become part of my existence. Kevin told me to be grateful, since things could be a whole lot worse than they were. I never questioned what that meant. I learned to be a good worker no matter how tired I was, if only to keep Kevin in the better mood.

CHAPTER SIXTEEN

❖◆❖

Finding Faith

1987 (25 Years Old)

Kevin wanted to keep me as physically fit as possible. He encouraged me to jump on a small jogging trampoline during the hours I was not doing manual labor. He never wanted me to rest! He said that if I laid around, I would become lazy. He kept me on vitamins every day and I was not allowed to have salt or sweets except for the occasional treat. I went to a dentist in Mexico and my doctor was a Mexican pharmacist. I recall when I first began seeing the pharmacist. It didn't matter how good my health was, some things you can't stop from happening. The visit was by my own request. That's when I was "officially" diagnosed with asthma by Yolanda, the pharmacist, and was given my first prescription strength inhaler. That was in the aftermath of an anaphylactic reaction that almost took my life.

For the first five years I was with Kevin, I suffered frequent asthma attacks with no relief. He would purchase me cough syrup or give me a swig of tequila and tell me, "you'll be just fine!" When I was in a full-blown asthma attack I'd get on my hands and knees and try my best to stay as calm as possible. I wanted to cry because I was afraid, but knew I couldn't since my bronchiole tubes constricted my breathing. Sometimes it would take hours for the wheezing to subside and it would leave me exhausted with sore lungs.

I remember the fast relief I experienced the first time he bought me an over-the-counter inhaler. I fought the urge to be angry with Kevin for having made me go through years of attacks without one!

I also learned that an inhaler is of no use if it isn't close by when caught in an asthma attack!

One hot summer day on the west Texas property where we were building the house, my life almost ended.

We had been busy working all day inside the house, since it was so hot outside. We were laying rocks with mortar around the bathtub. The unfinished flooring had gaps in it that opened to the crawl space beneath the house. Kevin and I had both just taken showers with a make-shift bucket on a rope and I was not yet dressed. Just below where I was standing, a skunk was roaming under the house and I must have startled it. The pungent odor of its spray suddenly rose through those openings of the flooring. It was toward the end of the day, and I was very tired. I had just begun to dress when the smell sent me into the worst attack I'd ever experienced. Immediate anaphylactic shock occurred with the startling accompaniment of spasms throughout my bronchiole tubes and the back of my throat. I wanted so badly to say something, but truly had no breath with which to speak!

Kevin was inside the house with me, but he was useless since he had no clue what had happened. He only knew there was a bad smell, which he commented about, but he had finished dressing and was absorbed with another project and didn't know about my predicament. I knew my inhaler was in the camper that we were still basically living in, but I didn't have enough breath nor time to tell him I needed it. I knew right away that this attack was different than anything that had ever happened before!

The only option was for me to go get the inhaler myself, but the scalding hot ground outside was full of cacti and sharp rocks and I could never walk outside barefoot. I was desperate. The fog started to roll into my vision and I was unable to see colors. I tried calmly to finish putting on my clothes. But it was getting worse. I put my shorts on backwards and inside out, and then I couldn't zip them. I put on my dirty shirt, inside out as well, that I had taken off before bathing. I felt the coolness of mud slide over my skin, but it didn't matter. Nothing mattered, except to get to that inhaler. Everything was turning white. But I still needed shoes on! I knelt to put them on and it was almost more than I could do to stand back up again.

Still unable to speak to Kevin, I began my eternal journey across the floor, and out the backdoor, to the patio. I told myself I was almost there, but just as I began to relax, the hammer fell.

As I made my way across the hand-laid brick patio, two things happened. First, I reached out into the air in front of me and my hand faded away into the solid white that now completely surrounded me. Second, I lost the feeling in my legs. I picked up one leg and placed it in front of the other. My normally smooth gait was now transformed into a mechanical jerking movement. I had no muscles, no synovial fluid inside the joints, only bones to carry me.

In my desperation, I began praying for God's help.

> In my distress I called to the Lord; I cried to my God for help. From His temple He heard my voice; My cry came before Him, into His ears.
> Psalm 18:6

I thought of nothing but of God and angels. All I could do was silently believe that I had not suffered through this life just to end up dying on that scorching ground beneath my feet, all alone, without my family. In my oxygen-deprived state I prayed to God to come and rescue me.

Please dear God, I give my life to you. Please don't let me die, not now, not like this. Please God, I beg you to save me. Carry me, I'm so tired. I'm so scared. I cannot see, please come to me, and help me Lord, Please!

During those prayers, I had left the back porch and turned right, sliding my right hand across the entire length of the backside of the house. It was about sixty feet to the camper. The door was as high up as the gate on a pickup truck. With a power I did not have, I pulled myself up into the camper. I recalled an overall effortless feeling seeping through what was left of my consciousness. It was as though someone else was carrying me.

Crawling with my body of bones, I could not even lift my head. Somehow, I made it to the bed and blindly reached up with my hand, immediately feeling the bag. I pulled it to the floor. Miraculously, the one thing I needed fell out of the purse and against my fingertips, the inhaler. I could not see anything.

I knew in my shock and blindness, that an angel had handed it to me.

With my trembling hands, I put the pump to my mouth and squeezed. I repeated it again, but my breath was weak. I wanted so badly to cry but if I had, I would have died. I knew without a doubt, I had to be strong and fight that battle.

The moment I took those first puffs, I followed the instruction once seen in a commercial. Silently, I counted to fifteen. *One, two, three, four, five, six, seven, eight, nine.* My colorless vision started coming into view. *Ten, eleven.* My vision started taking on color. *Twelve, thirteen, fourteen, fifteen.* I felt a surge of life in my chest! My lungs ignited with a gush of oxygen.

God had resuscitated life back into my lungs! *I'm alive!* I cheered mentally, as my first exhalation came with a stream of tears. Knowing a higher power had just saved me, I sat in a tearful silence in the air-conditioned camper and communed with Christ for a moment. It was His moment to shine for the mercy and grace He showed me on that day. He was filling me up with His sweet love. I contemplated why I hadn't put my faith in Christ before that day. I sat and thought of how real He and His angels were.

I reflected on how I had just experienced a miracle. As I'd made my way to the camper, I knew that God had heard me calling out His name. The whiteness of my vision, I knew, had been the clothing of the angels who were sent to rescue me. In my state of complete blindness, I could feel them as they carried me to safety.

God had ordained a supernatural event to happen and I alone was His captive audience. I felt so spiritually connected to Him. He rescued me when I was at my weakest, just before death!

He would find a way to get me out of that place, someday, and back with my family! I now had a reason to believe!

> "My grace is sufficient for you,
> for my power is made perfect in weakness."
> 2 Corinthians 12:9

Later, I told Kevin about the asthma attack experience, but not the God experience. I didn't give him the details about my struggle, mostly because I felt that he would not be interested in knowing about it. Kevin didn't believe in God. And angels.

I asked that I be allowed to see a Mexican pharmacist. Everything we did was in the town across the border. The American town we lived in was much too small to have pharmacies and doctor's offices.

I meditated on the love that I'd experienced that day. The very experience that almost took my life was also a lesson that taught me to believe, have faith, and that there was hope for me. That is when God and His angels had heard my cries and had rescued me, way out in that west Texas town.

CHAPTER SEVENTEEN

Desperate for Love

1988 (25 Years Old)

It was 1988 and we were staying with Kevin's grandparents on our annual Florida trip. Other extended family members had come and gone for the day, and his grandparents had gone to the store. Kevin called me into the family room, back behind the kitchen. He told me to sit on the floor at his feet. I was never sure about his mood, so I always tried to err on the side of caution, careful not to make him mad. I could sense that his voice was almost playful with me, like he was teasing me. My love-starved self-hoped for any attention he was willing to show.

He challenged me to talk about my life growing up. "Did your parents appear to love you? What was their favorite thing to do with you?" I started talking enthusiastically! I thought he must be interested in my answers. I began talking about my daddy and when I used to go fishing with him. But just the memory made me miss him so much that tears began falling from my eyes, and I asked "can I please go to see them just one more time, Kevin? I promise to not ask again. I won't even stay the whole 45 minutes. Just once more? Could I please go, please?"

The smile suddenly faded from his face. Just as clouds roll in quickly to form a stormy sky, so too Kevin's mood changed abruptly.

His seated posture became more erect. Something I said had set him off; it was so difficult to know what not to say to this man. "You're an ungrateful bitch!" he yelled. I jumped up from my spot on the floor.

He was out of his recliner in a second.

Whoosh... Kevin's hand missed my head as I jerked it back. He moved forward and swung again. I dodged the next one too. I heard the whine of the air as his hand missed. He was enraged that I moved away.

With tight lips, he demanded me to "come here! NOW!"

I hesitated as his face turned beet red and his lips curled down on the corners. Slowly, I approached him.

My heart was racing with the horror and I begged, "please Kevin, I don't have to go see my daddy. I'm sorry I got carried away. I miss him is all. Please, you asked me . . ." As I got closer to him he reached out and snatched the collar of my t-shirt and crimped it up in his fist, making the neck tighter and tighter.

"I will teach you not to ask for those people again! Do you understand what I'm saying to you? When will you learn? They are not your family! They do not love you! They never loved you! They don't want anything to do with you and you belong to me! You have no family! You don't hear them knocking on the door, do you? I OWN you, do you hear me?!"

He began palm slapping my face as I tried to loosen his grip on my shirt! Terror filled every nerve in my body. He punched me in the face, then he forcefully slung me like a ragdoll across the room. I felt the momentum and tried my best to grab at something, but it seemed the room itself was spinning with me. It happened too fast for me to get my hands out in front. I saw the rocking chair approaching. I recall hearing the thunderous crack as my head hit the wood. There was no pain; my body numbed as everything went black.

The next thing I remembered, I woke up to his grandmother spoon-feeding me soup. She handed me three pills to take and then she insisted I finish the soup. My head hurt so badly! The air seemed smoky. His grandmother coaxed me to drink iced tea through a straw. I did as I was told, laid back, closed my eyes, and was out again.

I woke again, and saw that it was daylight. Incredible pain in my lower abdomen had jolted me out of my coma-like existence. I cringed at the intensity of it. Grabbing the full length of the starched gown I had on, I scooted across the bed to the side. I called out for someone, but there were no noises to indicate anyone else was even home. The pain, again, gripped at my organs like rotating blades that were ripping me to shreds! I tried to suppress a yell, but the searing pain only intensified and shoved a scream out of me.

Still, no one came. I felt light-headed as I began to push myself off the edge of the bed to a standing position. Then, in a flash, another surge of pain griped at my insides and I thought I would faint. I crossed the small room to the door. Terror-stricken, I opened the door and yelled for someone to "please, come, please!" I knew something bad was happening, and it was not my imagination. This was real, and I didn't know how much more of it I could take. I fought the pulsations of brain-frying pain, slamming the door shut just as a gush of bodily fluid, and other, pushed its way past my underclothes, and onto the floor. I was horrified.

I saw it! Right there in front of me! All over the wooden tongue and groove flooring! I could see everything. My responsive gasp was the sharpest breath I could muster. The wholeness of it all over-took my tortured soul. I lifted my head up long enough to catch a glimpse of my bruised and battered face in the mirror, just before falling to the floor.

Again, I awoke on several more occasions to more sweet tea, soup, and pills. Then I saw Kevin. He woke me out of my sleep and lead me to the bathroom for a shower. He told me to get ready to come to the table for dinner. After he left me, I looked in the mirror and was frightened by what I saw in my eyes. The bruises were faded pale yellow and barely visible, very different from the day before. But how could that be? Had I only imagined seeing an image of a bruised and battered face? Looking at my reflection, I saw something else was there, dark circles around my eyes, from sickness? My skin was an ashen color. I reached up to touch the fading bruise on my cheek and orbital bone area, immediately wincing at the lingering tenderness. I showered and put on the gown that Kevin had laid out for me. I felt so emptied inside. Different than hunger for food, no, it was an emptiness of emotion. I wondered, *what happened to me? Why am I here? Why won't he just let me go. Why does he keep me?*

Kevin and his grandparents acted like their usual selves, as though nothing at all had even happened.

It is true, I am doomed to this life. How Lord, do I pull myself out of this hell?

Kevin told me of my misfortune right in front of his grandparents. "You should be glad you're not bringing that baby into this world. It would've messed up your body. You would have gotten stretch marks, just like my ex-wife did! I'd no longer want to look at you! You'd be no good to me after that. Just keep that in mind if you go getting yourself pregnant again! Besides, the baby would've totally been yours to take care of anyways! I would've had nothing to do with it." He also told me that I had gotten a fever afterwards and was very sick.

Later on, with no one else around to witness the affection, Kevin hugged me and told me that he was very sorry for what he did. He said he didn't understand why he was so angry that day and he promised to never lay his hands on me again like that. "Tammie, you have to be a good girl."

I silently thought if he said another word, the built-up nausea gurgling in the pit of my stomach, would become projectile, and he would be the target. I silently mused, *I guess that'd piss you off real good, now wouldn't it?* Laughing at him mentally seemed to help lift my spirits. Whatever it took to bring me peace. I had learned how important peace was to my mental state.

There were days in which I felt like a rock lying at the bottom of the ocean. Too heavy to lift my own head up. I hadn't even known I was pregnant. I knew that I had lost it because of what Kevin had done to me. That is what dominated my thoughts as I lay in the bedroom for days, dissecting details about what happened, and why. There was not to be any resolution, I could clearly see that. One day I awoke at his grandparent's house knowing that I had to move on just to move at all.

Though it was tough to take in, I was determined to put the loss behind me. Kevin told me I was his love and he couldn't wait to take me swimming in the ocean, or lake, or wherever I wanted to go.

To think that I'd believed this man was normal! Or was I the one not so normal? How would I know about love or normalcy anyways? I couldn't even remember much of my life before I was 15. I had been with this man for so much of my life!

I was forever stuck in his world of abuse. But I wanted to hold onto faith! I had to keep hoping that one day I would be free or that one day I'd become the woman he dreamed of. I couldn't dwell on my slavery, for it would certainly eat me alive if I did.

I reflected on how much I had learned about survival and keeping myself calm. My heart always danced in my own fantasy world of the fake love that he gave to me. Kevin was the man whom I had hoped to someday become woman enough for. When I first met him, I was weak, just a girl. I had seen the other side, the world without someone to protect me. The world without his love which, as fragmented and confusing as it was, somehow still brought small windows of nourishment to my broken soul. The scars that I carried long before Kevin and Texas, still clung to me. I was desperate for the love he was willing to give, even though that love occasionally turned violent. Still, I was willing to wait for that light of hope once more.

CHAPTER EIGHTEEN

The Grandfather

1988 (26 Years Old)

That same year we found ourselves, once again, in Florida visiting Kevin's grandparents. This was a rare occasion that we returned to Florida twice on the same year.

It was during this visit that Kevin decided to leave me at their house for an entire two weeks. He said something about "important business" he'd needed to take care of. He needed to drive back to Texas alone.

He had never left me at his grandparents' house before. My family lived a mere forty-five-minute drive away! Kevin told me that he would be gone for a week. I was shocked that he left me there! After that week had passed, he called and told his grandfather to give me the message he had been delayed. That extra week made all the difference. I became frustrated staying at these people's house whom I didn't know, except through Kevin, and he wasn't there. I was very uncomfortable. I stayed by myself in the back bedroom. These people did not make me feel welcomed; his grandmother didn't anyway.

For many years, the grandfather was the only person besides Kevin who spoke with me. He tried to be funny and at times he made me laugh. He was comical looking with his constant plastered smile. He was always nice to me and I was tempted to think he loved me as a granddaughter.

That all changed.

During the start of that second week there, the real grandfather came out of hiding, the one that I never knew. I could see that he was the same old man on the outside but the person inside was different than the day before.

I would never forget that foggy morning, just before dawn. He came into my bedroom as I was sleeping and I felt the weight of the covers being lifted off me. As he began touching my stomach, I just laid there. I wasn't sure if I was dreaming. Then I suddenly knew what was happening. I woke up completely and saw the faint image of Kevin's grandfather over me! I abruptly pushed his hand away, closing my eyes so I didn't have to see that face again! He attempted once more to touch me, and I shoved his hand away with a demanding "NO!"

He left and never came back inside my room again. But I had learned my lesson and I locked the door from then on. That ruined all the respect and love that I once had for him. My heart was really shattered. I had allowed myself to love him as I would my own grandfather, for eleven long years, I thought he loved me as a granddaughter-in-law. I even called them Mama Jo and Grandpop, though I always knew it was pretend. For me, I needed something to believe in. Some fantasy of thought that I was loved.

As I laid there I mourned for what I never really had: the man whom I had thought of as my own grandfather.

When Kevin finally came back to get me, I told him what had happened and all the emotions that went along with it. I told him how much it affected my heart and that I'd thought of that man as a grandfather all those years, and now I never could again. But Kevin had been completely unaffected by the story.

He had arrived back from Texas with no explanation of where he had been or what his business was. All he said was that he had been back to Texas. It didn't matter what he was doing. In my opinion, there was no excuse that could be good enough for leaving me at that place for so long, or even at all!

I got the weirdest feeling from Kevin. It was like he had been renewed somehow. He had on different clothes: stylish jeans, New Balance sneakers, and a designer t-shirt! He had a new haircut and his face glowed. He got mad when I asked, saying that he just needed new clothes! Of course, I didn't take that opportunity to complain that I wore rags from thrift stores. I concluded that the man had changed! Maybe the journey itself was something that he somehow really needed. I left it at that.

I told him that I didn't want to ever be left there again and that if I were to be left someplace, I would stay on that hill in Texas for however long he needed! He had left me there plenty of times before. Still, in the pit of my stomach I sensed a difference in Kevin. Something had changed in him during those two weeks, that he was not willing to share with me. Not that I remotely expected him to.

CHAPTER NINETEEN

Protective Bubble

1988 (26 Years Old)

As Kevin's violence grew more frequent and became stronger, I fought to save my inner self. I was my own advocate. I had to fight for the soul I had living inside of me. I refused to allow him to strip me of my youthfulness and tranquility of mind. I continued living in a constant state of unpredictable emotional and physical turmoil. I desperately needed a safety net, and that's when I created an image of a "protective bubble." No matter what words he used to tear down my innocence, no matter the physical or sexual abuse, or my intense fear of being left alone, there inside that bubble, I found refuge.

It was a state of mind. As I imagined going inside that place, it brought comfort to me. I could shut out anything else going on. When I needed to be relieved from my anxiety, panic or fear, I closed my mind off and went to that place of calm. It glowed with a brilliant beam of baby blue light. It had a slight vibration to it to soothe my nervous system and calm me down.

Life was so complicated to me. Really, it was throughout my entire life. I had a relationship with God, though I never really understood it as that. I knew He was there. He was my defender who kept me alive. He was my overseer. He watched what happened to me, as He guided me.

I lived to experience nature's own happiness. Just seeing a roadrunner sprinting with its toothpick legs across the floor of the desert with a baby snake in its mouth, gave me that chance to giggle with him, and smile that he had caught dinner.

I often wondered if leaving the desert would create a void in my soul. I had become the desert's daughter. I promised myself to never forget it. I would carry the desert with me wherever I went, and it would stay living inside me forever.

I prayed for freedom under the moon but I believed the ultimate virtue was patience. My existence was so bland and colorless, that joy came in hearing the whistling canyons of the mountainside. There was so much that I'd missed out on as a young adult. I began to believe my existence there in that desert had a deeper meaning not yet revealed to me.

My environment was the most serene, peaceful place, and its stillness created its own melody in my mind. The violin bow swayed and whined gently on the wingtip of the golden eagle as he soared over my head. As the sun took refuge in the abyss of the west, so worn-out and fatigued from its day's shine, the melodic sounds of a piano played on. There, in the stillness of the canyons, the winded current of the native Indian bamboo flute whooshed through the empty arroyos, sweeping and searching. Still, silence hung across the mountain range that stood far above the heat dance and blur of the lonely desert floor.

I stood on the edge of my solitary hill, with blank eyes staring. I was focused on the earth's scent that was so peaceful and calm; that scent of white sage, blue bonnets, and perhaps a hint of rain in the air. There was the unmistakable smell of dirt and possibly an animal carcass somewhere in the distant hills. The wind carried the odors across the land.

I often thought of the similarity of the terrain to that surrounding Jerusalem, that place where Jesus had stood. That land connected me to him.

"We need to find God, and He cannot be found in noise and restlessness. God is the friend of silence. See how nature—trees, flowers, grass—grows in silence; see the stars, the moon and the sun, how they move in silence…. We need silence to be able to touch souls."

– Mother Teresa

I never once found myself in danger in my twelve years of desert living, apart, that is, from the very person who brought me there! I did once encounter a poor rattlesnake which was not, as it should have been, hibernating in the winter months. I was walking in my rock garden when the rattles started shaking just under the edge of a cactus plant. So, I shot it with my pistol. Three times. I couldn't figure out why it was still trying to get away.

I once adopted a pack of wild dogs while living in that house. There were four of them all together. Kevin took money out of his monthly stipend to purchase a large cheap bag of dogfood for them. Bob Barker was my favorite. He was a blue tick hound dog that barked all the time when he came to the hill. I guessed that he thought the best thing he could do in exchange for the feed I gave them, was to keep the hill secure from intruders. Those dogs would show up and sleep for days, then they would be gone for weeks, sometimes months. Poor Bob came back alone one day. Kevin said Bob had heartworms. Bob was convulsing and grinding his teeth so hard I could hear them breaking in his mouth. I begged for Kevin to do something to end his suffering. So, he took the pistol and shot him. Before, I always tried to never cry, since Kevin always said that it showed weakness. But losing Bob and knowing he suffered, ripped out my heart and I cried a lot on that day.

The last time I remembered a human dying, was when I was fourteen, and my grandpa had died of lung cancer. It had been eleven years since then. My grandma had died while I was gone, but that just didn't seem real to me.

Bob Barker and the other three dogs were the first animals that were mine, besides a kitten named Twinkles when I was a little girl and my horses; Champ and Charlie. Technically, the wild dogs were not mine; they belonged to the open range. But I still loved them. They loved me too. I picked many ticks off those desert animals!

My more content days in the desert were when I remembered to speak to God. He took me in as the child I was. I had no knowledge of Him and His disciples and their stories in the Bible. I didn't know God but I could feel His presence there, in my lonely desert. I felt that I knew the most important basics of morality. Don't lie, don't kill, don't steal. Don't use the Lord's name in vain, and if you hear someone else use it, immediately go in prayer for that person's soul! Something else I took to the desert from my childhood, was my habit of saying the nighttime prayers Momma had taught me as a young girl. I always said that same prayer. It ended "…and please make me a good person. Amen."

That life was confusing to me as a young woman growing up isolated from the outside world. I didn't know my purpose, nor myself. *Who am I? Why am I here?*

I'd go to sleep and awaken to a whole new day. I never woke up burdened with yesterday's thoughts. It was my own rule. Falling into full-blown depression over my situation was never *ever* an option. Sure, I was sad many times. Yet, to have allowed myself to fall into a victim mentality, could've been disastrous for me. I would just lie down in the desert and become the dust itself. It was a frightening thought. To lose all hope would've been equal to surrendering myself fully to Kevin. I found refuge within my protective bubble of existence.

No, I always tried to be uplifting and have a happy soul! It seems my "protective bubble" was more than just a barrier against destruction but also a soul renewal system!

Kevin also sought after some level of peace from the earth. He embraced the mud baths and the hot springs of the Rio Grande. Those experiences invigorated my soul and kept my inner person still, quiet, and restful. It was Kevin who taught me about nature and how I should always take the time to "stop and listen." Or was that my daddy? I really couldn't remember some things very well at all. It didn't matter really. It had become who I was, and I knew that I'd be that same person for always, regardless of where I'd heard it from! It was the only lesson that made sense to me.

The sun shone on that hill every morning as it peeped over the line of the mountains, so clear and crisp. It made the beveled glass on my handmade windows cast flashy rainbows all over the walls. The moon would be there to greet me every night, with as many stars as could fit into one sky.

The connection I had with the desert afforded me the spirit to smile. At times, I still felt loneliness, anger for being separated from my family, hurt from the violent assaults, and pain from the lies in my life. I frequently found refuge inside my soul-preserving bubble, which kept reality from damaging my inner core. I established a unique type of calm that took anything remotely good, and made it appear inconceivably beautiful. I knew that the little girl in me, the one Kevin took away from her family, was still there. He believed he owned me, but the truth is, he never did.

CHAPTER TWENTY

Well, Call me a Basket of Wildflowers!

1989 (27 Years Old)

One morning I woke up early and cleaned the house on the hill as best I could, since it was still under construction. Kevin was gone away, as he was a lot. Mornings were the best time of day in the desert! I was enjoying the solitude of the countryside at dawn. Mexico was two miles away by car through town, or one mile across the farmlands by foot. As the sun rose, so did the traffic. From my place at the front living room window, I could see the dust billowing in the distance as the farm trucks left the paved roads, kicking up a dusty trail between the onion and cantaloupe fields. Across the landscape to the right, far off on the dusty pink horizon, rising dust clouds indicated that Mexico was waking up too.

My mind wondered as I steeped my first cup of perfectly-blended tea leaves. Smelling its fresh rich aroma took me back to Mexico's west coast, where I was first introduced to this delicious blend. Just as I started to take the first sip of the day, I thought I heard something. We never got visitors. Never. I thought it must be Kevin.

I looked out of the window to see a taxicab. It had just made its way up the steep rock driveway. A pregnant woman got out of the cab. As the cab waited, she came up onto the front porch and knocked. She knocked again.

I was in a funk. I tried to imagine who this woman was. I didn't remember having met her. Not that I'd met anyone in town! I wondered what she wanted. Just as the woman was about to turn away from the unanswered door, I opened it...

"Yes, may I help you?" I asked.

The woman spoke no English. "Buenos dias," she said. She proceeded in Spanish, "I am looking for the owner of that Mustang, Kevin." The woman gestured outside where our Mustang was parked. Actually, Kevin had bought it as an apology gift for something he had done to me.

The woman was very short, with thick jet-black hair that fell down her back and was gathered at the crown of her head with a barrette. Her skin was darker than most Mexicans I had seen, since they usually shielded their faces. I had been in Mexico enough to deduce that she was from the interior of her country verses borderline residency. The woman seemed to be about eight or nine months pregnant. She was very proper and proud as she informed me with a broad smile, "I am Tatiana. I am Kevin's wife."

I had to think fast to keep my jaw from dropping in shock. A surge of saliva quickly formed in my mouth and my stomach began making loud growling sounds. No, this was no ordinary situation. I had an explosive urge to throw up right on the floor. I struggled to maintain my composure so that this woman would not see she was upsetting to me. At that point, I had to know more. I had to figure out how to get more information, and pray that I could handle it.

"Welcome! Come on inside. I am family, tell me all about it." I asked if the lady minded if I sent her cab away, so we could have time to chat. With a curt "claro que si" (yes, of course) from Tatiana, I gave the "hi-ho" for the cab to leave. It was good that I spoke enough conversational Spanish to communicate with her.

I was not at all in my comfort zone. I desperately wanted to hear how Kevin had pulled this off. But I was starting to wonder just how seriously twisted the situation was. It's funny that I didn't even consider doubting Kevin's guilt.

"Amazing stained-glass windows," Tatiana said in Spanish. "What beautiful colors from the sun!"

Yeah, whatever, I was thinking. *What are you really here for? What are you seeking? You're pregnant and looking for the man I've lived with for half my life!*

I thanked her for the compliment. "It's very nice to meet you. I am Kevin's cousin, Tammie." I willed a warm smile to my face, "So you and Kevin are married? That's so exciting for you! Congratulations!"

The woman spoke with enthusiasm, "I am so happy to finally meet his family. We got married in Conchos. Almost the entire town was at our wedding."

I responded with "please, have a seat and I will get us some iced tea."

I disappeared behind the wall of my back-porch kitchen. I thought I might have a heart attack any minute. I immediately grabbed a small paper bag and cupped it around my mouth so I could slow my breathing. I began brainstorming. *He left me at his grandparents' house only a few months back! Was that when they married?* He had spoken in the past of how he never wanted me to have a baby, since it would mess up my body. He had told me many times that he would get me a child one day, and it would be mine, but that I may have to live with certain standards for that to work. I never had a clue what he was talking about, so I always blew it off.

"Hope you like sweet tea. That's what our family drinks! Kevin is away on business for a few more days, so sorry you've missed him." The woman grimaced at my statement, accepting the tea. She was oblivious to her surroundings, as well as my stony expressions. I thought, *Our family? Bah! We have no family together, and we never will!*

"Oh, that's too bad that he is not here. Well, at least I got to meet his cousin!" Tatiana made the announcement with tender regret. "I was able to cross the border with our marriage license. The patrols issued me a visa that is good for just one day. But my Kevin will get that all straightened out and I can become a US citizen. I just love my new house! My friends want to come help me decorate it!"

I mustered a smile and remembered to be polite, "Well, tell me all about the wedding! Did you get married in a church?"

"We had a huge wedding! My family paid for everything. All my relatives were there and my friends. Kevin's parents were unable to make it, but they gave thousands, according to what Kevin said, to help us build our life together . . . We were blessed with so many gifts and cash presents. I am a bookkeeper and all my coworkers from Los Polamos School were there as well! My best friends want to come here to America, to help me decorate my new home!" She looked at me and laughed. "I guess I already said that! You must understand, I've waited so long! Kevin wouldn't bring me over here. Are you here visiting Kevin?"

She got up from where she was seated and began to look around, asking if she could look at her home. Her mouth didn't stop.

As she returned to her seat on our newly-upholstered Duncan Phyfe sofa, she continued. "He doesn't know that I got this one-day visa to come across the border, I was going to surprise him. I haven't seen him in over three weeks! Is he okay? I worry when I am not with my new husband. I don't ever want to lose him, being so far away makes me miss him even more. He gives me butterflies in my stomach. He is so excited about us being pregnant with twins! I can't wait to see my Kevin! Tell me again, Tammie, where is he?"

I never once had the chance to say a word. As she continued, I felt as though I might pass out. This was such a shock! It made my insides shiver like I was cold. Surely the story was all true. I had three days before his return from the city. Perhaps that would be enough time to calm down and think rationally. Probably not. If this woman was telling the truth, I knew my time on the hill was limited.

I was very careful not to show my emotions or my overwhelming nausea to Tatiana. My stomach was making audible churning sounds and my insides twisted painfully. I knew it was time to use my neighbor's phone to hail this woman a cab, and get her off the property. That woman had disturbed the peaceful flow of my morning.

In a flash, my life had changed! Isn't that what I'd been praying for all along? For something to happen?

I didn't want to leave the woman alone in my home, so I took her to my Mexican neighbor's house with me. When the neighbor, Maria, opened her front door, I bolted in the house, closing the door behind me, to ask if I could make the local call for a cab. I had left Tatiana standing in the shade of the overhang of Maria's front porch.

After I made the call, we returned to the cooler temperatures of my living room to wait for her cab. Tatiana continued chatting away about her new love, and the wedding, and the babies.

My head had begun to swim. A torturous ache had started creeping up the base of my neck, and was working its way over the curve of my skull. I hoped that the taxi would miraculously grow wings and arrive immediately. I could no longer concentrate on anything that came out of that woman's mouth. What did Tatiana expect to find, showing up unannounced at Kevin's house? I couldn't really be suspicious of this woman though. She was only looking for her "new husband" and was pregnant with his twin babies. It wasn't her fault. I didn't want to be rude or be the cause of her going into pre-term labor right there in my living room!

Finally, I answered one of many questions, "I live here with Kevin. It's a family thing, you know."

Yeah, I thought to myself, *you have no idea what a messed up little marriage you really have and I for one, am not about to be the one to tell you.*

CHAPTER TWENTY-ONE

The Night Before Telling Him

1989 (27 Years Old)

How do I even begin the conversation? "Oh, your wife came by"? Or "oh, I met your wife"? Or "oh, by the way, I know that you are married to a Mexican woman, who is carrying your twin babies"? Quite frankly, he must be crazy to think I would never find out. He probably wasn't planning to keep it secret forever. But this confrontation was something I had to do. She knew that I knew, and that made it real. This was going to cause such an abrupt change of my life. I now had to figure out Plan B.

Since the woman had showed up at my house looking for her husband, I'd hardly slept a solid hour! I had used the neighbor's phone three days ago to call Tatiana's taxi to return her to Mexico. Thank the Lord her visa was only good for one day. I don't know what I would've done otherwise!

That night, I had sat in shock. I sat in darkness, thinking. I did the same thing for the next three days after that taxi had driven away. I didn't want to tell him. I hated to think of that conversation's outcome! Things always had a tendency of becoming my fault. I wanted to be with my family back east in Florida more now than ever before. If this was all true—and I believed it was—going back to them was the only out, the thing I had spent a lifetime asking God for.

I didn't know anything about being on my own. America had become the foreign country to me. I had not listened to American music in about ten years, apart from listening to the radio on our occasional trips. I didn't know anything about politics or football. I did learn some things from listening to Paul Harvey's 10 PM broadcast by myself sitting out in the pickup truck. I had lost touch on how to socialize in English. Or rather, how to socialize at all.

I was socially handicapped. I had never been to any bridal showers, though I did witness one wedding. I never went to a prom, graduation, or concert. Only once had I gone to Disney World. That was in the 5th grade when my friend and her family took me. I didn't even know how to cook anything other than beans and rice. I had lost years of my life all spent in the desert with a man thirteen years my senior. I'd been with Kevin since I was 14, left with him for Texas at 15, and now I was 27. All I'd ever known about being a grown up, was in being with him! I felt so lost and alone.

His lies had always been consistent. He had them memorized from the very beginning. Perhaps some of what he said had some truth in it. He'd say so many things like, "your family never loved you! They never came, did they?"

I would lie to myself too, saying that my life was not that bad. When in truth, I had absolutely nothing to compare my life to. After so many years of being kept away from other people, I didn't really know what kind of life real adults led. For some reason, unknown to me at the time, I had believed that I was sent by God. For that reason alone, how terribly wrong could my presence in that desert be? I found myself turning more to God in my most desperate times.

Who am I? Come, God, speak to me! Whistle your flute softly into my heart! Bring it to Your earthbound child! Give me hope! Love me for me, God!! Whisper your guidance and show me the way out of this mess.

I sat thinking of love and what it had meant to me. I was a simple woman. I had never asked for a miracle. My image of the world was created through the books I'd read and the life of meditations in the desert alone. Love was all I had ever really wanted. And so, I wrote in the dim light of the flickering candle:

> "Love is free. Love is not in a hurry. Love teaches you to stop and listen to silence. Love overcomes sadness, and despair. Love glorifies your unknown storage of strength. It builds a mountain of prosperity and energy. Love is within the soul of every human. Love doesn't mean a person or a place, but it's that clarity of image that brings sunshine to one's soul, leaving one feeling nourished, wholesome, complete. As simple as that."

The night before Kevin returned, while I sat in the darkness, the silence was almost deafening. I listened for his truck tires on the gravel. I remembered feeling so angry, so frustrated, and so incredibly hurt. I felt one hundred percent alone. My despair was worse than it had been the entire twelve years I had been with him.

The purpose of Kevin's abuse and manipulation was to leave me scared of where I would be without him. Through the years, I had to build my inner strength so I could survive in his make-believe world. I became disciplined. I had to be a calm person to avoid his physical assaults.

I never quite understood the abuse or the statements that I wasn't as good as he and his family. He tried beating me down, but deep inside I knew I was innocent. Kevin fought with his own demons. I was just caught in the middle of his battle. He attempted to convince me that he was a "real man," when really, he was only a piece of a man.

As my life played out in my mind, I realized that, no matter how bad the abuse was, it could get worse. I did everything I could humanly do to avoid angering him!

I could hear the whistling wind approaching. I knew when a front was passing through by the abrupt storms that would dip down the slope of our valley. It would begin with an incredible blast of wind and sometimes the temperatures would plummet.

The howling of those winds grew louder the closer they got. That sound always terrified me. Memories of childhood scary movies made me afraid of a lot of things up on that hill, alone. It would take me days to recover from the tension in my muscles and lack of sleep. The pistol never left my side.

This fear and helplessness had been my life, day after day, for years.

That night before Kevin's return, I remained on the couch, curled up in the corner with pillows and the pistol. I tried to sleep and not see the face of that woman. I kept dreaming of running as fast as I could. The beating of my own heart pounded loudly in my ears. I thought I would die if I didn't hurry and wake up.

I opened my eyes to the morning light and wondered, if only for a moment, if it was all just one big nightmare! But I knew better. This waking life *was* the nightmare. As I was thinking this, I heard the truck tires on the rocks outside coming up the hill to the house.

He was home!

CHAPTER TWENTY-TWO

Train Ride with Satan

1989 (27 Years Old)

Kevin pulled up and jumped out of his truck. He was excited from his journey to the civilized world. I wondered if he even had another woman in the town where he always went. I contemplated for a moment. *He had never allowed me to join him on these trips. I had never even been to that town.*

He came in the front door and began talking to me as I lay on the couch. I had a ballcap on my head covering my eyes, as though I were asleep. He talked anyway, from the kitchen area. When he came back through he reached forward to nudge me and said my name. I was scared and thought, *I don't want to show him how mad I am because it will start something that I can't control.*

"Tammie! Are you okay? What's wrong with you? Answer me!" I took off my cap and revealed my bloodshot, dark-circled, swollen eyes.

He gasped. "What happened to you? Was someone here? Did anyone bother you? Why do you look like someone just died?"

All I could say was, "a pregnant woman came over the other day." I silently commended myself, *good. Stay calm. Stay in control.*

He asked without hesitation, "who? A woman? Pregnant? Well, what did she want? What did she say?"

But I had already lost control. Now he was standing over me, hands on hips, waiting for *me* to answer *him*!

"It was your Tatiana, Kevin." I looked straight into his eyes and said, "how could you possibly think I'd never find out? You're a dog! I am leaving! I want to go home!" This is the part where I was losing control of my mouth, spilling out words I had held back for days.

I always knew by his thin lips that his rage was coming. His stare would become hypnotic. His posture became more erect. More tense!

He came at me before I could respond and hit me across my face.

"What home? This is the only home you'll ever have! You no longer have family back in Florida! Remember, they gave you to me!" He was yelling at me. "What did you say to my wife? I thought I made myself clear long ago that you were not to speak to anyone! Answering the door was off limits and you know that! Why did you answer that door?"

He grabbed a handful of my hair, and with a tight hold, he said in a shaken voice, "if anything happens to her or those babies, it will all be your fault! Do I make myself clear enough, Tammie?"

I felt like a piece of porcelain china, so fragile. Yet, knowing how Kevin fed on my weakness, I held my chin up to his and responded cautiously, "I told her that I was your cousin and I encouraged her to give all the details. Yes, she and I sat talking for hours on the couch. We drank tea."

I realized how tired I was. "Your pregnant wife told me so much that I haven't slept in three days."

His anger immediately faded, he released his fist grip on my hair as he became…happy? It made my stomach churn. He stood back from me with his head tilted and folded his arms up high on his proud chest. "So, what did you think of her? She can be your friend!"

I turned and glared at him but he seemed so far away from me. This was all so very much to put on my shoulders. I was still in shock just from that woman showing up at my front door!

I struggled to say something significant, anything at all really, but the only word I could muster was, "What?"

He smiled as though he were announcing some great news to me. "Yes, I told you that I'd get you a baby and a friend! Aren't you excited? I mean, all you do is complain that you don't have a baby and you have no friends to talk to! Well, I have fixed all that!"

Is he freaking kidding me? I thought. The baby I wanted was to come from my own womb, not the womb from another woman. *What is he talking about?* I searched for the undiscoverable answer. He'd never let me have even one friend. This was all wrong!

He continued, "since things are now in the open, I will share all my plans! I need to go and get her tomorrow, and she will stay the night with us. You can go ahead and be my cousin. You will sleep outside in the camper and I will share our bedroom with her upstairs."

He went on with his well thought out plan. "Then we'll take a train trip to Conchos, the next day, all three of us! There's a fair we can go to! How exciting, huh? We're going to stay the night there in a hotel and we'll come back home the day after that."

I spoke before I thought. "Kevin! Are you freaking kidding me? I mean, you really think I'm going to go along with this craziness?"

But he wasn't even mad. He explained my new life to me in his terms. "You will not complain because it was you who wanted a child and a friend. I did all of this just for you, just to make you happy. She will be your friend and you will be the mother to the twin babies that she will bring into this world." He continued, "you must be patient and understanding with her."

He kept going on and on, confusing me more with every word. I questioned my own sanity. I was silently feeling as though I was in a war zone. The bombs were going off and I was bleeding internally. I could feel the open wounds, the slashed arteries, and the splattering blood. I felt the rivers of nausea rushing up my esophagus as I held my hand to my mouth and ran out the door. Bending over the side of the porch I dry heaved. But I had absolutely nothing in my stomach. I couldn't even recall the last time I'd eaten. I wiped my mouth with the backside of my forearm, and went back inside. I drank some water.

Kevin continued, "Tammie this is all my property, my house, and I warn you, you're nothing without me! If you even try to leave, I'm telling you right now how this will happen! I'll kick your ass first. Then kick your ass out that door! You are thousands of miles out in the middle of nowhere! You will NOT succeed in leaving by foot through that desert! And you will NOT be allowed back into MY house ever again!"

I had no choice but to go along with his insidious plan. I was in shock, and my thoughts became robotic. I made it through a day of Tatiana staying at our house, or rather, in Kevin's house, while I was reduced to staying in the camper outside, alone! By now the old bread truck camper was even more old and run-down.

Kevin's plan was to tear away at my strengths and convince me again that I belonged to him or to no one. He had me so far out in the desert without money or a car I had no other options available to me.

But I knew the time for me to finally be done was near. I always asked God for my freedom and I had always been patient in waiting. This peculiar scenario, though, was testing all my resolve. I knew I had to leave soon. I had to figure out a plan and I had to keep my composure. What had happened there on that hill was the unforgivable. It had been an entire lifetime of unforgivable. My heart couldn't take anymore. This sin of Kevin's was larger than my whole life lived on that hill. Maybe someday I could learn to forgive him, but that would be in a whole different chapter of my life!

For now, I was a silent storm brewing. I would never again look at him the same. I was forever scarred by his senseless act of self-indulgence, or whatever title one could put on that act. *It's all so very dumb anyway*, I thought. He already had a woman who was there to give him everything but he traded that in for an unknown. *Or maybe he's known this Mexican woman for a long time.* I knew that I had never fully understood the man who had been my only constant for all these years.

I thought I'd experienced the worst of the storm, but it looked like it had only been the prelude.

That first morning with Tatiana began with everyone meeting up in the back-porch kitchen in search of coffee. I still had dark puffy circles around my eyes since I still hadn't slept. As hard as I tried, I couldn't hold back the tormented tears all night long.

Before going in the house that morning, I had gone for a long walk on the hill, trying to rid myself of the stench of lies surrounding the property that no amount of soap and water would remove. I finally regained my composure, somewhat. I couldn't think about where Kevin and Tatiana had slept, or what they did before and after they slept. Just the thought made me want to change into something I never was. Crazy with jealousy. And why?

In the kitchen that morning Tatiana asked Kevin, "what is wrong with her? Why is she crying so much and why will she not speak to me in Spanish anymore?"

He kept blowing off her questions and speaking to me in English, which upset and confused Tatiana even more. "What's wrong with you? You look like shit!" He sneered at me. "I thought I told you what my expectations of you were! You need to go wash that face of yours or do something!"

I was in no mood for him. "I don't want to play this game. I told you, I want to leave."

He broke into my sentence with a calm, firm tone. "If I need to take you into that camper, she is going to wonder what's going on! If I need to I will, and you can be assured that I will beat your ass so badly and make you stay here while I take her into Mexico! Do you hear what I'm telling you?"

In my misery and mental turmoil, I didn't answer. I didn't want to be there anymore and just didn't know how to leave!

"If you do not answer me, I will drag you by the roots of your hair into that camper! Now answer me and tell me you understand!" He grunted at me.

"Fine!" That was all I was willing to give.

"I want you to go and get yourself looking better than what you look like right now! We will be leaving in an hour."

I retreated to the camper. I was thinking of how the trip to Conchos was going to work. I knew there was a state fair there and I'd never been on a train ride before. Although my excitement for the journey ahead was distorted by my troubles, I took the time to think. I hadn't been to a fair or carnival since I was a young girl.

Apparently, the two love birds had been hanging out there quite a bit. Tatiana said it was her hometown. Kevin had said that they were not going to visit her family or friends. He had told Tatiana no when she'd asked. They needed to pick up some papers from an office when they got there. She asked him again, begging to take me too so her family could meet his family. He told her again forcefully "No!" He would return to the city with her later, once they dropped me back off at home in the States the following day. He told her that I wasn't well, that I had been feeling sick. That way they could have lots of time with her family! Every time she asked, "what's wrong with Tammie?" he just told her again that I was sick.

He always thought I couldn't understand what he was saying in Spanish and I never told him otherwise.

I felt like the second hand on a clock, ticking aimlessly away. In the blink of an eye, we were in Mexico and on the ancient railroad train. There were always children, no matter where I went, they flocked to be near me. I was seated with children on both sides of me, as well on the bench seat facing me. Across the aisle and facing me was Kevin and Tatiana. With as much love and attention as the little children were showing me, all I could think of was them.

Don't look! I told myself. So I kept my eyes on the dirty train floor. All hope was lost. Tatiana spoke to Kevin about her confusion as to why I no longer cared to speak to her. I didn't care to listen anymore to their conversations and concerns.

I wanted to get lost in the moment, this was my first train ride ever and it was even going through the interior of Mexico! I wanted so badly to make this a significant moment.

So many times, I would begin to relax a bit and then my eyes would uncontrollably trace across for a glance. *Oh no! They're kissing!* He would have her embraced in his arms, gazing into her eyes.

Once, as I was absorbing the blow of the invisible punch, Tatiana jerked her head around and caught me looking. I tried to hide my eyes from everyone, especially Tatiana. I'd cope with it all for now, if only out of human concern for her pregnancy. I'd find my way out of this tragedy soon, very soon. Patience is a virtue but I was losing hope of being able to stay sane in their presence. He never showed that kind of attention to me; it wasn't in his character. At least I'd never believed it was. What was wrong with me? What point was he trying to make? Was he trying to torture me?

Then out of nowhere I remembered it. Back when he was beginning his manipulation tactics on me, back before my parents had allowed me to go with him, he *was* like that with me! Had it all been fake? My whole existence with him was one big lie. I have been nothing to him but his captive victim all this time, too afraid of his wrath to go against him and leave.

We got off the train in the town of Conchos. I dragged my heart behind me, while I watched the two love birds all day and into the evening, holding hands, kissing, and giggling. Every time Tatiana glanced at me she would look confused and again Kevin would tell her that I wasn't feeling well. I wanted to yell the truth! Venom was trying to force its way up and out of my mouth. Every moment became more difficult. Every time they exchanged gestures of endearment, I grew closer to an all-out breakdown.

We walked through the state fair all afternoon. Kevin even threw baseballs, winning stuffed animals for his pudgy bride while she giggled and lifted her little foot when she kissed him. I constantly retreated to a bathhouse to dry heave! We headed for the town center. The air was thick, hot, and muggy. Then, as if my heart hadn't been dumped on enough, I thought I'd heard the word "hotel."

I hadn't even thought of this! Or had he said this to me before and I blocked it out? The reality was stomping on my heart. Now I was ready to just lose what mind I had left!

"Please, let's take the train back now!" I begged him.

The heat of the situation was raised to an all-time high! I followed behind them, after several attempts to reason with him. This was the most emotionally painful experience I could remember yet in my life!

Perhaps I could run to the police station to ask for help getting back to the States? Yeah, Mexican Federales were not exactly known as the most empathetic people! Then what? To the border? What about a ride to the house? Even if I knew how to get there, then what? He had the only set of keys, and there were burglar bars on the windows! Then what? He had all the money. I had not a cent after twelve years, I didn't even own a collection of change! It was hopeless! Reasoning with that man was pointless. He had his own agenda and he was not going to be swayed by any woman! My hate and disgust was as putrid as though he threw me inside a dumpster filled with rotten spoiled food and animal parts!

In the hotel room there were two full sized beds. Kevin gestured for me to take the one bed over by the window and that the other would be for him and his beloved! I knew that I would not be able to dislodge the walnut from my throat!

All I could think of was that I had lost. I no longer existed as Kevin's anything! Not that I ever was. I had always clinged to that shred of imaginary love he gave me: little pockets of hope from an occasional sign of love. Whatever affections I had convinced myself Kevin felt for me were gone. It was official, I was nobody's anything!

While Tatiana was in the bathroom getting herself ready for his bed, he came at me. He held me to the wall and, with his lips curled tightly inward, and eyebrows scrunched together, he warned me fiercely. If I interrupted their peace and caused those babies harm, I would live to regret it!

"I will ruin you forever! You understand what I'm saying to you? I will hurt you worse than I have EVER hurt you before! Do you hear me? You will lay your ass on that bed and go to sleep and behave like a normal person! I am sick and tired of your complaining face! I pay your way! I put food in your stomach! You should be kissing my feet for what I do for you! You understand what I'm saying to you? I will kick your ass so badly! I mean it Tammie!"

I just stared at him in total belief. Trembling under his grip, I knew he meant what he said! He had earned that from me! I feared for my own life. I did not answer him before she came out, nor blinked an eye in my shock. I shook internally, knowing that his threats had moved to a different level. I truly felt he would take my life if I crossed him. In the same breath I didn't believe I could last much longer in this emotional state he placed me in. It was as though I had become a ticking bomb. The moment of losing control was not far off and I would surely explode regardless of these threats he made!

I couldn't stop from hearing the giggles and the motion of the covers and the groans and kisses in the darkened room. I thought he must be doing this to me to see how far he could push me or to desensitize me to my new life. Or maybe he got some sick pleasure somehow by knowing I was in the other bed hearing it all!

I could tell he began trying to have sex with her, despite her verbal protests! I couldn't take it. I screeched out, "really Kevin? Don't do this to me!"

He said nothing back, as his focus was now on her.

Tatiana kept saying "no, no, Tammie is here! You're hurting me, Kevin. Stop!" He could care less what she said, he did what he wanted to do to everyone!

I could no longer compose myself! I promptly ejected myself from the bed. I left the hotel room in only my pajamas, despite Kevin's demanding shout to "get back in that bed -NOW!"

I stood in the quiet breezeway of the hotel somewhere in the interior of Mexico. A dot on a map. A forgotten soul. I cried for all that I wasn't. I cried for all that I carried, the years of pain that lay trapped in the folds of my mind. I cried like I had waited my whole life for this event to spill the tears of a shame I didn't know how to undo. I felt pity when I looked at myself. I felt disappointment for not having any control of my own life! I cried to wash the smell out of my head, out of my memory, of the garbage I left in that room. The trashy man I ended up with.

Finally, after I cried until there were no more tears, I returned to the room, and decided to try and get rest. I had not slept an entire night in many weeks.

The nightmares took me to the dimly-lit path of my life. I was walking too fast and my feet were bleeding, leaving bloody prints. I could smell my blood. The monster would find me! Where were my shoes? I was on a cliff, seeing the river flowing so far below that it seemed like a tiny brook. I heard something. Here it comes! I could feel the warmth of its breath on my bare shoulder! I was terrified that it would take a bite or claw at me. I had no choice, so I jumped!

And suddenly, I wasn't falling! I was gliding! It wasn't a bad dream after all! God granted me serenity and I gracefully flew to a secure place where He comforted and embraced my soul. He heard my sorrow! And I slept. *Oh my God*, I prayed. *What have I done to deserve your presence all the way inside my dream?*

> For I am the LORD your God who
> takes hold of your right hand and says
> to you, "Do not fear; I will help you."
> Isaiah 41:13

I slept a restful sleep. I felt God's presence! But just as the thought of his presence was strongest, the thought left me. I was not strong enough nor disciplined enough to live in my faith and knowledge of God at that time. Though He left my conscious mind during waking hours, he shielded me still as I continued to tackle my battle of life. He quieted my soul.

The following day, I ignored everything. I realized that I had to get ahold of myself. We returned to the train station and then rode the old train back the ninety-mile ride. As far as I knew, I could've been the only person on the train that day, since all I did was hug the window. All I ever wanted was to be happy and loved, to be appreciated and wanted. All I ever knew had just vanished away and was lost forever.

Tatiana stayed in Mexico, while Kevin accompanied me back home to the hill. He stayed overnight, then he was gone again the next morning. The next time I saw him, he said, he would have the babies and wife in tow. That is, if I had not already found a way out by then.

CHAPTER TWENTY-THREE

Stockholm Syndrome

1989 (27 Years Old)

My best memories were of when we first met and I fell in love with Kevin. He had so much power over my mind and environment. No one was there to contradict his brainwashing and how he filled my head with such lies! I came to believe that this life was normal. He told me I must be grateful to him for having saved me when he did and that I would have been nothing without him! That is what he always said to me.

In my dreams Kevin was the man I loved. He had taught me to believe that he was my protector who would fight anything just to keep me safe. "Trust in me," were the words behind every kiss, every put-down, every blow.

I was just a girl. Though this man was never my answer from God, he created in my mind an image of himself as a god-figure for me to latch onto. He was consumed with satisfying his pedophile lusts, and I did not know, nor did I have the maturity to fully understand just how sick he was. In the beginning he bought me pretty things. He gave me drugs and wanted me to dance for him. He told me that I was his sweet girl. He told me that he would guide me into a more peaceful existence. He would create a safe haven that would be our home forever. His touch was gentle as he coaxed me with tender words.

I had no reason not to believe in his storybook tale. No reason, except for that one window of my mind through which the real Kevin was slowly being revealed. In time, I learned that there were three sides to Kevin: the master con artist whose name was untainted in the community, the master manipulator who fed on young girls, and, worst of all, the abuser, violent and unrelenting.

Kevin was so very reassuring. "No worries for you, my Tammie. I will teach you how to live the life of Mother Earth. All that you know from your past will disappear someday, as new memories of our love and life experiences will replace it. You'll forget all about those people who falsely lead you to believe that they loved you. Trust in me, Tammie, I will never fail you. Trust in me, I will never hurt you. They don't love you, sweet Tammie. They don't deserve to have you. Trust in my love, I will bring you nothing but joy. I want to teach you all that I know and more."

I had to believe him; he had become my everything. Over time I gave up asking, "how do I get myself out of this abusive situation?" and changed it to "how can I not disappoint him, and just bring him happiness. He loves me so much." Time revealed his violent tendencies, and with that came fresh assaults. I learned to take minimal risks. I learned to love and receive love from the environment around me. I could sit for hours looking across the waters of Lake Amistad or sitting on the banks of the Rio Grande. In the seclusion of the desert, the open farm lands were my peace with the magnificent mountains in the distance that separated me from the other culture, just beyond the ridge of that same mountain range.

But now I had woken up. I finally realized the painful change that now faced me. Kevin had burned the candle out. An unyielding darkness had been formed out of his self-indulgence. I now understood more of my life, that it was nothing but a distorted illusion. With that realization came the ticking of the clock. My time on that hill was about to end. Change was a new word for me. My life had been a constant for twelve years and I had remained the same as well. Yet, my introduction to change, initiated by Kevin himself, had ignited the possibility that the world was not what I thought. All this time I had believed, without questioning, what Kevin had taught me. But now I suspected every word he'd ever spoken was a lie. He was no longer credible. Was my entire life nothing but a lie? Had he deceived me for all those years? What about the time he left me at his grandparent's house for over two weeks? It had been a "business trip." That happened just before we returned to Texas and he left me again to travel into Mexico. Is that when they married? Were his grandparents in on knowing what was going on? Had he made a complete fool out of me, all this time? Hadn't he done that to me all my life? I felt so much shame as all the realizations flooded my once-thoughtless mind!

I realized that God was finally answering my many prayers for freedom. I knew the disconnection from Kevin would be painful and it would take much courage and resilience. He had conned me into believing he was the best of all worlds. I only hoped that in my final days on the hill, I would have that opportunity to tell him exactly how I felt about being mistreated. I wanted to tell him that he would never have that chance ever again to cause me distress, pain, or any kind of suffering. It would be much easier if I could fast forward to who I'd someday become. I embraced the music that God himself played inside my heart. I inwardly smiled at what being "finally freed" would feel like to my soul.

CHAPTER TWENTY-FOUR

Courage and Resilience

1989 (27 Years Old)

I had begged on my knees for Kevin not to go to Mexico, back to Tatiana, to have the babies. Better yet, not leave me by myself at home. Something was telling me that he was going to be gone a long time. I asked if there was someone in Mexico I could stay with. I was desperate since I'd never gotten over my terror of being there on the hill alone. Nothing would sway his decisions once he'd made them. He was going to Conchos to be with his new bride for the scheduled induction. He was excited about becoming a new dad to the twins she was carrying, and he kept saying how he was not sure why I was not as excited since they were my babies, not hers! That they wouldn't be hers for long.

So the darkness, the sounds, the nightmares, the immigrants passing through in the night, the fear, they all were mine alone to battle through. On top of all that was the isolation with its intense loneliness.

But surely that was the least of my worries. There were bigger things to think about. I knew that movement on my part had to be well-orchestrated, since I was hundreds of miles in the Texas desert lands and well over a thousand miles from my real home. I wasn't certain how to even do it. I needed a lot of prayer for God to somehow tell me when, how, and with what non-existent money I would make my getaway.

The town was two miles away and I had never been allowed to venture there alone. I had never even left the hill by myself. For twelve years I was subservient, handicapped, and dependent.

As the days of Kevin's absence turned into weeks, I lost track of how much time I sat staring out at the mountain range. I emptied everything out of my head, just to see what nothing really felt like. I forgot my existence and my energy. Nothingness was satisfying because it took away the pain. Nothingness felt good.

I stayed as calm and collected as I could during those next couple of weeks. Eight days was the longest he had ever left me before. By day fifteen there was still no sign of him and my supplies were growing thin, as was my body. I had stopped eating a long time before that. A bite here and there was all I could stomach.

At times I wondered if something had happened to him. If he was even still alive. He would never have done this to me before. He wouldn't have been gone for weeks! But perhaps he was turning to an even darker side and, regardless of Tatiana, he would have eventually forgotten me. That's how I was feeling. Forgotten.

I would lay with the gun in my hand as darkness fell on the open plain. I was certain that God would give me visible guidance. For now, I was in a survival mode. I wanted something to knock me over the head, or perhaps even for God himself to say,

> "my daughter Tammie, it is time
> to go now, get up and go and trust
> in me that I will do the rest."

Guidance was the one thing I prayed for. I thought that as long as I did feel the presence of God's hand, I knew I'd be okay. So that's what I waited for.

Why was I playing into his sick game? Just as I had done before, I questioned my sanity. What kind of person does this to someone?

I couldn't even ask to go home to my family, for fear of retribution. What kind of life would I be able to live after freeing myself from his chains? If I was so afraid to stay alone, how would I be able to live alone outside of his protection, or rather, his control?

I didn't have the experience of being independent. I didn't know anything about holding down a job. He had let me work in the beginning as a waitress once or twice, even as a tour guide. But they were short jobs.

I didn't even know how to relate to people in a social setting. I didn't know how to make adult decisions. What if I was able to somehow break free and something bad happened to me before I was able to make it home? What if he, by chance and miracle, gave me a car to leave with and something broke on my car as I drove out of town? What if someone was nice to me, would I know how to not appear so gullible? How was I to know how to not stand out in a crowd? Even the word "crowd" made my heart rate increase.

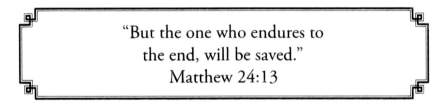

"But the one who endures to
the end, will be saved."
Matthew 24:13

I sat, day in and day out, looking out of that front window through the burglar bars and across the valley. I wasn't sure I was ready to make it on my own. Being left behind scared me. It felt like a test of my ability to make life and death decisions. It just seemed so cruel.

I had just enough water left for about two more days but that would be it! I had already stopped taking sponge baths a week ago.

The Mustang sat on the hill, but that didn't really matter since he took the keys when he left. When I ran out of water completely, I'd have to walk into town with a couple of smaller bottles, which I had never done before. I still had a small amount of beans and rice to eat.

These recent events had changed the way I saw Kevin. It had changed the way I saw everything, including myself. My life felt like a fairy tale. Not real. It was never mine. None of it. I somehow felt that I was a Cinderella, only I was kept by a more sinister human than the old step-mother ever was.

I had always been disposable to Kevin. Tatiana was now his new and ultimate prize. She was his way into the Mexican family, culture, mafia, power, or whatever he was seeking across that border.

I never found true comfort in his bed anyway! When the house started coming together, after years of construction and hard labor, the bed had been placed below the Bermuda hip on the second floor. There, above the bed, was the big beautiful triangular-shaped fixed window of intricately hand-crafted stained glass of a quarter moon and stars. This was artwork that was created by my hands. After that first day that Tatiana arrived at the house on the hill, I never again slept in that bed.

Kevin was wrong for expecting me to live like that.

On day 17, I sipped the water from the bottom of the last blue barrel. Perhaps a half of a cup was left. I knew that I was in desperate straits. My very life was now dependent on my courage to leave the property, against his orders. Having to take that trip into town by foot meant that people would see me. He would know I had gone.

I pulled out Kevin's oversized backpack and loaded it with three one-gallon jugs. One of the jugs had my half cup of water, which would get me to town. I put on jeans, a plaid long-sleeved shirt, boots, and a ballcap with my hair pulled back and tucked away from view. Then I stuck my hand under the old truck engine compartment for some dark grease. I rubbed the grease and dirt on my face to camouflage my fair complexion. I figured I was as ready as I'd ever be for my journey into town.

It was essential that no one saw me as a woman. Especially a white woman was sure to be recognized, and perhaps someone would tell Kevin. The town had a population of 1250 Mexicans and two

Americans. So, I was really trying not to stick out. I would've loved to spread the news of what was happening on top of that hill to tell some of those townspeople, but I feared Kevin's temper! I had learned to respect a private existence, just as he demanded.

CHAPTER TWENTY-FIVE

Kevin: The Evil One

1989 (27 Years Old)

My two-mile walk to the nearest gas station for water had been uneventful. No one had been suspicious, that I could tell. I poured water from the hose on the side of the building into my three-gallon jugs and walked all the way back to that hill. I would have endured my life of slavery for many more years had Tatiana never come into Kevin's life. I feared Kevin's wrath, his threats of more beatings, when I'd ask to go to my family's. That same fear never allowed for a wondering mind of drifting to thoughts of permanently leaving. Also, I depended so much on Kevin's knowledge of life and living, that I never considered leaving as an option.

Time had simply stood still for twelve long years. With this sudden change in my life, I allowed myself a moment of grieving. Kevin's selfishness made me angry, as he ripped my self-image apart at the seams.

That afternoon I had heard gravel under car tires. Kevin had finally returned home! I remembered looking outside and thinking, *how am I going to do this, Lord? I don't know how to leave! What will I be given to leave in? Will he give me money?*

That is when I saw the unthinkable! Kevin had brought that woman back to our hill! Somehow, I think a part of me was in denial that it would actually happen. He *had* told me that *was* the plan, but I refused to believe in the unbelievable truth. My heart started thumping! I couldn't breathe! I felt myself go numb and I was overcome with such sadness. I had held sadness and depression away from me for all those years, afraid of it and what it would do to me. There was a black velvet curtain lowering on me. I couldn't resist it. It was too heavy to push away!

I silently cursed at myself for not having left earlier, however impossible it would have been. *Now what am I to do? What am I going to say?* I had not planned for this! This wasn't even on the list of possibilities!

Kevin got out first and walked around to the other side of truck. He opened the door for her and took the baby, cradling her in the nook of one arm, while helping Tatiana out of the truck with his other free arm.

As I just stood there at the window, I watched my world end. I looked straight into the eyes of Satan as he laughed in my face! He told me to look at Kevin's precious family walking up to his house. Everything Satan stood for, anger, frustration, horror, jealousy, retaliation, became what I wanted so badly to feel at that moment. I was petrified of that feeling. It was like a balled-up fist wrapped with thorns twisting inside my throat.

"Tammie!" Kevin called out to me.

I couldn't answer. I had nothing good to say. I was in perilous times. There was no deeper hate than what I now felt for Kevin. No other urge could overcome the growing venom in my heart. Any minute I would fall into oblivion!

God! Are you even here? WHAT CAN I DO? HELP ME GOD! I'M SUFFERING GOD! PLEASE, GOD, I NEED TO CALM DOWN! I pleaded with the one I'd known in my desert life. I waited for another voice to squeeze through my atmosphere, as Kevin kept calling my name and looking for me.

"Oh! There you are! Come in here, I have someone I want you to meet!" Kevin said proudly. He said it as though this were perfectly normal.

"Tammie, what's wrong with you? Why are you so red? I thought I told you not to be outside during the day! Wipe that bewildered look off your face and come with me right now." Kevin was stern.

Without saying a word, I followed.

I had not even seen a baby in far too many years to even remember. There it was, all cradled in Tatiana's arms as she was nestled in my seat on the couch. Kevin took the baby from Tatiana's arms and placed her in my arms. It was so little. It smelled of lotion. In my head a storm brewed. Two forces of such exchange they equaled the other in power. The forces of love and hate battled for dominance over me.

The baby was so cushiony and soft. The atmosphere was frozen as I looked at it and then looked up and asked, "I thought there were two?"

"The other baby didn't make it." Kevin said sadly.

My face was emotionless as I cradled the baby in my arms. I handed her back to Kevin. I turned my body and went to the kitchen to boil water for some tea.

Nothing. I felt nothing. I was stunned at Kevin's powers to destroy me. I had nowhere to go nor any way to get there. I had no energy left to fight against him. My guess was that this was Kevin's sick solution for my desire to have a child and a friend. The other guess is that he'd grown tired of me and needed a new life. Yet it made no sense, I would have been willing to just leave!

I steeped my hot tea, removed the bag, and took a sip. Ah, the warmth running down my throat coaxed the tension away.

Finally, ready for a woman to man discussion, I entered the living room. The baby already had a crib there, and she was laying in it quietly. I turned to the couch and there they were, embraced and kissing!

"How can you do this to me?" I blurted angrily.

"Tammie, stop your nonsense right now! You are in my house and will show respect!" Kevin's lips were tightening.

I had already put the cup of tea down. My stomach was gurgling with hunger, anger, and fear. How did he think I could handle such an abrupt change as this?

He glared at me daring me to say anything more. Tatiana playfully threw her leg over his, took his face in her hands, and began kissing him. He moaned and suddenly this was the worst day of my life.

Both their eyes were closed in their passion. I was simply no longer human. I did the only thing I could to make them stop. I reached inside the crib and gave a little pinch to the little baby on the thigh, and moved away quickly. I felt it was taking one for the team, because they needed to stop. It wasn't healthy for me to be put through this.

Little baby let out a huge wail. I was pained by what I had just done but I just had no other way to make them stop!

Kevin pushed Tatiana away from him, as he lunged forward and gathered the baby in his arms, saying, "what did you do to her? Did you *pinch* my baby? How could you *do* that? Get out of here *right now*! GO!" As he pointed away from them.

I walked away quickly to the back-porch kitchen, relieved that they weren't kissing, and felt that the baby would be okay. I felt horrible but it had changed the atmosphere. So quickly and completely.

Kevin came to the back-porch kitchen and punched me in the face without even a pause! He announced that he and Tatiana were going back to Mexico to be around their friends and family.

"Oh no! You're not going to leave me here again by myself, are you? Please Kevin, don't leave me again! I'm so scared here alone in this house!" I pleaded with him. "I have nightmares every single night! Take me with you! I promise to be good!! I'm so sorry about the baby! It's just that, well, you shouldn't have been kissing her in front . . ."

Kevin turned on me like the brother of Satan. He slammed the side of my head with his fist. "Listen very closely to what I'm about to tell you. I am leaving you here, so you can get over your stupid little temper tantrum! My wife comes first now! Do you hear what I'm saying? She is *more* of a woman than you could have *ever dreamed* of being! You are a nothing! A grain of sand under *her* shoe! My wife needs to be in a nurturing environment, you dumb bitch. She *just* lost a baby! I will take her where we can be with people who can show us love! You sit your stupid ass right here! DO NOT GO OUTSIDE! Do you hear me?"

I was floored by his words. As weird and confusing and inconceivable as it all was, I'd always truly believed Kevin saw me as a girlfriend figure and that he loved me. Yet, in a flash, he finished off destroying the image of myself and of our pretend relationship. My world was a black hole and I was falling.

He and his little family packed up and left as I sat motionless in that same chair in the back-porch kitchen. Beaten, battered, and scorned. There was nothing left but the outline of where I once stood. The gravel crunched on the ground outside and I was alone once again.

He had said they were going to be with family and friends. He told me that he'd return in eight days. He had kept me prisoner for so many years I wouldn't even know how to have a friend. And family? Ha! I didn't know the meaning of the word at this point. What *was* the point to all this anyway?

I removed myself from that chair and walked to the quiet living room, where chaos had so recently unfolded.

I smoothed out my wrinkled mind by putting on a record from Kevin's 70's collection. That was the only music I had, besides Spanish music on the radio. I opened the windows to the afternoon breeze and stepped onto the front porch, facing the sun as it set over the mountains of Mexico. Leaving only the screen door to separate me from the sounds of music, I closed my eyes to the departing sun. Conjuring images from the sounds, I longed for the love described in "Sweet Baby James."

All this time, the love he had shone to me was a lie! It was all lies! Whatever I was to him I no longer wanted to be! He said that he had taken an ugly duckling and turned her into a beautiful swan! Lies! I was still an ugly duckling!

Kevin didn't know *who* I was as a person. I didn't even know who I was. Everything I saw and everything I was belonged to him. Yet, everything changed with Tatiana. I couldn't see clearly but my life was on a countdown. I only hoped that God Himself would show up and lead me out of that place I had lived for so many years. It was as though my legs were broken. How could I walk away, how would I know which way to go, let alone how to get there? And worse than anything else, how would I survive without him?

CHAPTER TWENTY-SIX

Mentally Preparing

1989 (27 Years Old)

Kevin had left to take Tatiana and her baby home to Mexico, but I was determined to be ready when he arrived back at the hill. I was desperate to spread my wings and take flight eastbound, back to Florida.

I always found hard work to do when I was upset. It was an outlet for my pain. Many times, I scrubbed my laundry so vigorously on the scrub board that my fingers bled. They would be raw for weeks! I would never even remember what I was doing, only that I was so upset!

It wasn't laundry that kept me busy on this occasion. I had eight straight days of anger and pain and utter devastation to fight through. I needed to get myself into shape, to prepare for the unknown road and the conditions on my journey back to the east coast. I jumped on the small aerobic trampoline for hours. I would stop to eat what little food I had and to sleep what little I slept.

I walked the property, finding the largest rocks I could lift and throwing them as far as I could, one after another. My enormous rock garden around the house was lined with rocks that I had specially selected on my long walks with Kevin in the desert. In my state of mind, I imagined Kevin on the receiving end, as I lifted each rock and threw with all my might. This had always been the place that I had had no choice but to make my home. Not anymore! I did not belong there! I picked up rock after rock and threw them far down the hill.

I meticulously thought through everything I wanted to say to him. I knew I needed to be strong and exude confidence when Kevin returned. I needed to have "the talk" with him, since no one else was there to do it for me. Facing the demon, my adversary, my enemy, my captor since childhood. That's how I finally saw it. That's how it was.

By day seven, I was out-of-my-mind crazy. I had to release the stress! I stood in the yard on the side of the house, at the lip of the hill. Blood was rushing through my veins and I couldn't get the image of them making out on the couch out of my head!

I walked very fast down the incline away from the house. Then I ran up the next incline, and began running across the desert floor as fast as I could! I left the protection of the house. I knew he forbade me from leaving the boundaries that he set up for me. But I no longer cared. I needed to get the stench of him off me!

I ran so far that when I finally stopped and looked around me, I found myself at the Rio Grande. It was a very secluded stretch of the American border. I'd crossed the main road a long way back, while absentmindedly running through the desert.

So! I thought, *this is what it is like to be free! Wow!* The temperature was in the mid-110s. I was so thirsty I wondered if it was okay to drink from the river. I was far from any town. I splashed my face and then I drank fiercely, as I was badly dehydrated! The experience of the rugged journey gave me a new kind of feeling of empowerment.

The warm breeze blew on my damp face. The stress of the past weeks was washing away in the cool swift current, across the rocks of the river bed. I could lounge on those cool rocks! The thought was so tempting. It would be the ultimate final treat for myself, before leaving the desert for good!

These thoughts were cut short. I heard something and looked up, squinting into the distance, as the view danced in the heat. Nothing. But 'nothing' could certainly turn into something very quickly. I had already spooked myself. There were mountainous canyons surrounding me, which echoed every little sound. Thanks to the stories I'd heard and horror flicks I watched as a child, I began imaging things, like a coyote, rattlesnake, or maybe even a hairless mutated canine that sucks the blood from its prey! The Mexicans call it the "Chupacabra!"

My breathing was increasing, and my fear multiplied as I attempted to get my bearings. I couldn't remember exactly how I got to the Rio Grande River. At this point I had the setting sun to guide me!

I ran faster than I'd ever run in my entire life. I stopped after what seemed about 30 minutes of running. The wind was beginning to whistle over the canyons and hills. I could see the miniature dust funnels far in the distance whipping down quickly, and then spiraling back up into the sky. I was running out of daylight as I reached the top of a hill, and I could see the house in the distance. I began running again, all I wanted was to be inside the protective walls. I was running so fast that my ears vibrated while straining to hear anything in the background.

My mind began drifting as I slowed my pace to a walk. Then I stopped. There was nothing here to protect me anymore. Nothing here really mattered to me anymore. I had begun my disconnection from that house. I would be there just one more night. *By this time tomorrow*, I thought, *I will have said my peace with Kevin and left town already. Surely that is what he expects me to do and will agree it is the best thing.*

I sat down on a rock, oblivious once more to the day's ending. Suddenly fear of an unknown canine lurking nearby just didn't matter anymore, as I gazed toward that little house on the hill. I had never thought that my own strengths or desires could make me an independent person. *What on earth am I going to do for myself, out in that big world?* I thought. *What has the rest of the world come to, since I have been living in seclusion? What should I know by now at my age?* This frightened the survivor mode right out of me.

I had been praying nonstop for years that God would help get me out of this. I felt that Tatiana and Kevin's new life was God answering my own prayers for freedom! I tried to let it all go so I could maintain my calm. Remembering the years of captivity had suddenly left me feeling claustrophobic.

Today was crushing in on me. But tomorrow? Well, that was going to be a different story.

◆

The eighth day, as I sat alone, rain shattered sideways into the four-foot tall stained-glass windows of the living room. It poured down as though the desert itself was crying, knowing that it was about to lose a daughter: me.

The deafening sound of the storm blowing by was calming to the soul. There was no question about my intentions now. I was sad and tired of thinking about the love I would have fought to the ends of the earth for, as confusing as that love always was. Even through the abuse, I believed that he loved me. I sat in my silence, trying to somehow *understand* that I had not belonged to Kevin's heart for all those years.

The reality of it hit me in the face like something sinister that challenged my sanity. I had put my life in the hands of a sociopathic pedophile. I needed to wrap my head around the fact that he was capable of even worse things. He was a violent man who was capable of murder. That crept through my thoughts, leaving me shivering at what I still had to face. Alone. As the rain came crashing down, I couldn't hear myself think. I wasn't even sure of my own thoughts anymore. He was all that I had for all those years.

The beauty of falling rain usually brought inspiration for relaxation. But this time, my mind had been filled with so much turmoil about how it would all play out upon Kevin's arrival home, that I barely heard the thunder roar in the skies.

> *Relax*, I heard a voice softly say in my thoughts. *Listen for the whispers in the wind.*

And I felt God's comforting powers.

I woke up hours later on the couch, lying on my back with the pistol on my stomach, and my finger on the trigger. I felt terribly confused about how I could even think Kevin would allow me to leave. The sun was beaming in from the front window as the light was captured in every prism of the beveled glass. I lay on the couch, watching in wonder as the familiar rainbow colors shot in all directions. Kevin was coming home on that day, or so he said. I continued watching the laser show, wondering who would be there to enjoy my artwork in years to come.

All the windows in the entire house were handmade, and created by me and my own design. Nothing had been done to that house without my help, my touch, since it took at least two people to accomplish most things. The living room with real wood parquet flooring, inset sliding doors, sunken bathroom with rock plastered around a three-foot-deep tub, all these Kevin could not have done without me. The hand-carved landing to a stairway railing had been removed from a hundred-year old house, and we'd hauled it on a flatbed from Florida as well as the 2X10 tongue & groove flooring upstairs that I helped lay across the beams. The Bermuda roofs had been dangerous to install, as I helped hold beams up in the air, while boards were attached and set in place. And then there was the 50-foot well, that I had been lowered into every day for months to carve out of hard Texas gravel and grit!

I had painstakingly laid brick as a rear patio. I remembered how Kevin had taken me to get four four-foot high stacks of brick from an old man down by the border. While he stood talking with the man, he told me to load the brick. I donned my gloves and loaded all the brick into the back of the work truck. Scorpions nested in the depths of the towers of brick, and it took me a while to transfer the load by hand. I always worked hard to please Kevin. He had me brainwashed into thinking that my reward for hard work was a small shadow of hope that he loved me. I would have worked until my fingers bled, if that's what it would've taken to please him. If I didn't work as hard, the verbal abuse would begin with "you're a loser," "your family gave you away," or "you're uneducated." Most damaging of all, he would say "you're nothing without me." I'd rather have spent a lifetime of never being praised for a *good job*, than to be beaten down over a non-truth that I believed as *the truth*.

I now had a clearer understanding of Kevin's feelings for me, thickly coated with muck as it was. Surely, he realized that I wasn't staying. Certainly, he wasn't going to give me a hard time. I had sat in days of darkness, inside the pain of his rejection.

As I dozed in and out of sleep, so many variables played inside my thoughts. It just wasn't fair. I had always been so addicted to what love he was willing to show me. But it couldn't have been love that I felt for him. *No.* It was weakness. *How am I going to have the courage to just walk away?* All my life he told me I wasn't strong enough to be on my own. As I sat there in a fog, I felt myself slipping into my old way of believing all that he said as the truth without question. Everything I'd always thought, I had been given permission to think. Didn't he own me? All this time he was right, I was no one by myself. I was a replica of him. Or was I?

I began thinking about how I was going to tell him. Whatever happened on this day, would be the catalyst for my departure.

I prayed so hard. "Please, God, be with me now more than ever! I need you now, Lord! Help me! I don't know what to do, what to say. I'm scared, God!"

I knew I had to confront Kevin, but I inwardly questioned, *would we both survive that very confrontation?* What would be his reaction once my own reaction materialized?

I dosed back off to sleep. When I woke up it was afternoon and I could see the barren farmlands across the valley. I would so miss this view! Just as I was feeling the fear build again, my stomach rumbled with hunger. I wasn't even sure if I'd eaten that day, as time blended and disappeared before me. My protective bubble no longer existed. I now felt everything, it was unavoidable pain, as I felt the weight of the world on my chest.

I gazed out the large front window as I left my seat on the couch. The light was casting long shadows toward the east across the vast, empty farmlands, as the sun was sliding down the western sky. I wondered how I could ever survive without the beauty that I'd grown to love in my American Jerusalem. I closed my eyes to capture that photo in my memory, of that serene love that nourished the valley and had always nourished me.

It seems Kevin wasn't even good for an accurate or reliable account of returning home. Another night was spent alone in the depths of my terror.

CHAPTER TWENTY-SEVEN

Surviving Kevin

1989 (27 Years Old)

Day nine.

Days melted into nights, and I never knew what time of the day it was. My restless dreams held on to every sound. I wasn't able to decipher between the patter of rain and other noises. My thoughts were frozen and so was my body. I couldn't move a muscle. Could it be invaders entering my house? What was that sound I heard in my dreams? I searched my mind for what seemed hours. Then it came to me, the familiar yet infrequent noise of gravel under truck tires as Kevin climbed the hill in his work truck. He was home! My heart started racing in my sleep! Wake up! Wake up!

My eyes flapped open to see the Smith & Wesson still in my lap. My finger was still on the trigger from sometime in my sleep when I had thought I'd heard footsteps on my front porch. Was it morning? My clothes felt damp from the daytime heat but I was confused. My life was much like a wild animal's in the great African Safari. I was trying to keep the predators away at all hours of the night and day.

This is the day, I thought. *I have to be strong-willed! Father, be with me now.*

I shuddered at the thought of having to be the one to tell him that I was going to be leaving. I somehow knew that I was a warrior that could conquer him, I only needed to find her someplace inside myself.

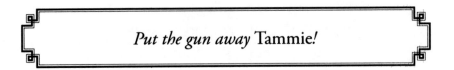

Put the gun away Tammie!

In the haze of my mind that fatherly comfort came, as God spoke His words.

I immediately slipped the gun into its holster, then into the box and under the couch it went. That is where I kept it hidden away during my hours at home alone.

Kevin entered the house. He seemed energetic and quite pleased with himself, as he began unloading things onto the floor. "So, how are you doing? Have you finished with the stained glass I wanted?" He began rambling, not even waiting for my response in between questions. I heard him in the back of my mind, but the things that were at the forefront of my mind, well, they drowned out everything else.

I knew the time was here, and that I had to confront this beast head on. Something told me he was not going to be happy. Something told me that he would be relieved. Something had told me before this day even came, not to say a word, but to just leave.

The night before I had prayed, "God, if you can hear me now, just tell me what to do, because honestly I'm afraid of my own decisions."

So, I began, "did you make sure that your new wife knows that she can't live here in our house? Is that why she's not with you? Did she protest when you left her in Mexico this time?" He stopped what he was doing and slowly turned from the front door to face me there on the couch.

With fire in his eyes and his chest rising as though he had been challenged to a fight, he said "you are never to speak of my wife with that tongue again, do we have an understanding here?"

Me. I was all alone in this fight and I had to face the inevitable. How was I to get his attention and do it right? Did I need to spit and hiss at him as a cat would to a dog? I had to think! I had needed to grow up long before this moment but never knew how. Time seemed to freeze my mind. I knew I must gain control of my warrior self and defeat my opponent with courage and grace. Then, if that didn't work, I would have to take the chance that he would hurt me.

I took a long deep breath, for I needed more oxygen to strengthen me! "I cannot keep this up, you understand. This is not good for me. This is not normal. My life with you has never been normal. You have kept me a prisoner on this hill for many years! I'm ready now to move on with my life. One that doesn't have you in it!"

He came at me before I knew it and embraced my small frame. He squeezed me tightly, saying with an eerie calmness, "now, now, you know my love for you is real, this is what you wanted! You wanted a baby and you will have to play by the rules for now in order for that baby to be yours. I will make sure she doesn't live here for long. It will be just long enough for me to get custody, so the baby can be all yours. You know I don't love her! I never did! It's all been a game to get the kid for you! I was doing all of this just for you, Tammie." I squirmed, trying desperately to break free from his man-tight embrace. He was hurting me.

I felt anxiety and panic rising up from my stomach, covering my chest like a dark black cloud, tightening my throat like a vise grip, tighter and tighter. I could no longer breathe. His embrace didn't allow for the expansion of my lungs. I closed my eyes and thought of the western sunset, the dark rich colors that changed as the sun crested the mountain range and sank into the earth. The beauty in the colors always filled my empty existence with warmth and hope. My body went limp. Relaxed...

He felt the release of resistance as he let me loose and he talked on nonchalantly. "See, I've been gone far too long away from home, I brought you some surprises from her family's house! They are so excited to meet you! Really, Tammie, you need to conform to this new life! I told you that you must live with it for only a little while!"

As he backed away I gasped deeply to fill my lungs. I sprang back from him and moved over to the front entrance, standing next to the very screen door I had made with my own hands. I had even burned his last name on the middle board. It wasn't my name! I was tired of his games! My heart ached with the burdens of too many painful memories of his abuse. I simply wanted to explode! I wanted to be set free! I was looking for his blessing to do just that! I had sailed across the worst of the raging seas, battled the biggest creatures in my nightmares, been beaten down emotional, spiritually, and battered to a pulp physically more times than I could possible count! I was exhausted, bewildered, and slowly becoming the aggressor. This life was no longer tolerable! He was bringing out a crazy side of myself that scared me! I was ready to be the victorious one, not him! He had pushed me out of my balanced mind. I was a loose rocket about to launch from its pad!

"STOP IT! STOP ALL THAT TALK! DO YOU HEAR _ME_? I won't put up with this anymore! I DON'T WANT TO BE HERE!! You have managed to _destroy_ my childhood! You _destroyed_ what I built here WITH MY OWN HANDS! This is your life, Kevin, not mine! You have mistreated me for most all my life! You have MADE ME live in a fantasy world that YOU MADE UP! This is not my fantasy! Not my dream! I am leaving, and you will give me money to do that!"

Kevin became animal as he leaped across the living room before I could open the door to escape. He slung me back across the room and onto the couch. He hovered over my body! His large hands wrapped around my neck. He began squeezing, as the cruelty distorted his face.

I was thinking in my state of hysteria, _he's gone insane!_

He was using my neck as a weapon to fling my head up and down against the side arm of the couch. Empty holes of darkness were striking lightning bolts across my vision. I felt myself going faint. I couldn't lose this battle! Not on this day! Not in this way! I pulled my knees in like a seated frog. I quickly positioned my feet in the middle of his chest.

I thought of nothing tranquil but of everything I had lost until I had nothing more to lose! No more being beaten up, bullied, and controlled! No more being kept away from civilization! No more being spoken to like a hired hand! No more words of thunder against my heritage, my beloved family!

I thought, *yeah, I love my family! No more, Mr. Big Mean Man! No more of your "my way or the highway" standards. No more pedophilia,* for I was still as innocent as a little girl in my mind! *No more wicked acts in front of others, like the violent blows or verbal insults and name calling in front of your family!* I brought to the surface of all these thoughts and more that had been bottled up deep within the latticework of my brain, deep inside my tender soul, deep into the subconscious mind just so I could survive. I brought up everything that had been stowed away for years. I rolled all these toxic thoughts into a ball, one that I created and only I could see and understand. It was the very expression of survival. It was "do this and don't die." For I finally knew without a doubt in my mind, this crazy man was trying to kill me! *I must survive!* His manipulation and intimidation tactics swam through my head. He had changed the rules! It was now kill or be killed!

The visions of my nightmares of that life as it was, with all its trauma and abuse, became a ball, a cloud, a sphere. It was airborne, and it went between my feet and his powerful chest. I had the power of God Himself feeding my quadriceps energy and pumping adrenaline through my body, as I forced my lungs to full capacity, and struck upward with my feet as I screamed to the top of my lungs, "GET OFF ME *NOW*!!!"

Backwards he flew, landing on one leg and against the window frame. He attempted to catch his balance but fell to the side and down onto the table that shattered many of his vintage music albums. I shuddered internally at what had just happened as I shrieked the highest, loudest scream I'd ever made in my entire life. On this night *God* had plucked a star from the sky and implanted it in my soul! He made me know that I was not someone to just throw away!

I quickly stood on top of that couch like it was my strong fortress! I did not back down, not having time to stop and understand that my strength was limited. On that night I did not care! This man had just tried to kill me, and I had saved my own life! With the help of the supernatural powers of heaven, I was sure of who I was at that very moment!

How dare he do this to me? After all I had done for *him* and all the patience and discipline I had shown him? After all that I had put up with! After all the fear he had created in me by representing himself as someone I dared not face in opposition against anything he said.

No more!

He stayed where he fell, in the darkness of his dim-lit misery. No one's hero anymore! "Who's the nothing now?" He didn't attempt to move a muscle. He *said nothing*. My concern for him had long perished, and I didn't question why he did not move. Perhaps it was that he had felt the full impact of defeat.

I gazed around the darkened room as I stood upon that couch. I spat out to him how vengeance could've been mine, if I had chosen to take it! Of all the evil that he had in himself that I could've easily claimed as my own power over him and his little wife!

I screamed these things at him out of my newfound knowledge! I told him he was a vacant human being! That he had no more power over me! That he held nothing on me that could change the knowledge I had now obtained! Knowing that he was a person lost in the devil's world, I stood down from my place on that couch and left his hill on foot.

I didn't understand how the day had become late evening. I barely noticed that I was even dressed or even how torn and tattered my clothes were. I barely noticed that I had literally walked into town. Into a neighborhood. I had only walked into town once before, when I went for water.

I came upon a neighborhood of small scattered adobe houses, in no particular arrangement. My world had become clouded over the moment I left that hill. I walked up and knocked on a random door. I was a walking zombie, not even in control of my own actions.

That house happened to belong to the attendant at the only convenient store in town. She was the only person who I ever saw in that town and there she was standing in front of me, eyes wide opened to this strange occurrence. She was waiting for *me* to speak. I couldn't remember why I'd knocked on this person's door. *On any person's door for that matter.*

"Please, come in," the young woman said.

In those years of desert living I'd only been inside the old woman's house behind my own, and that was only a couple of times. This small house was very empty. There was only a couch and a table with a TV on it. A small scenic picture hung by itself on the wall close to the TV. I was distant. I was holding onto every moment because I kept forgetting and drawing a blank to the very world around me.

I asked the polite girl, "where is the nearest pay phone?"

The girl directed me, "it's off to the left when you leave my front door, about a mile across the desert by foot, or two if you drive around on the main road. Are you okay? Would you like for me to get you help?"

"Help?" That sounded so foreign to me. I was the young woman who had been forbidden to converse with the population of that very town for half my life! I suddenly remembered that the first year there in that town, Kevin had let me play softball with the local women's league. That very girl had been there. She knew my face. When I had realized I didn't have the right clothes or even sneakers, I didn't want to go again. Every time I had run for a base, I'd tripped over my pants that were too long, or fell over rocks in my clunky boots. That was so long ago!

I told her, "no, I can make it just fine. Thank you."

The truth was I didn't believe in the word "help." I had no reason to believe there was safety in "help." At least not in that town. For now, the time had come to figure out where my plan A was taking me. I hadn't even drawn out a plan B.

I walked away, across the dusty marbled surface of the desert floor. I felt the coolness beneath the tender soles of my feet. I continued through the outskirts of the small town with a mere population of twelve-hundred and forty. Me, the American girl-woman, who lived with that American man who spoke fluent Spanish.

I walked in the direction my guide had given. The early evening had turned the sunset glow into a dismal grey. I reached the pay phone. I knew a few numbers by heart, though I hadn't called them for so many years. Without any thought, I made my first call. It was to *his* parent's house back in Florida.

I pushed "0" and then their ten-digit telephone number.

"This is the operator, how may I direct your call?"

"Collect from Tammie," I responded.

His mother, Sue Ellen, answered, "Yes, I accept the call! Hello! Is everything all right Tammie? Where is Kevin?"

In twelve long years, I had barely conversed with his mother and I'd certainly *never* called her collect!

"No, everything is *not* okay," I answered her.

The mother responded, "My God, Tammie, what's happened? Where is Kevin? Is he hurt?"

I thought for a second. I couldn't remember if I'd dreamed what happened! Was I dreaming now? I thought, he never moved after he fell. I couldn't remember if he *was* okay.

I had screamed at him. My own voice had terrified me! He had his hands around my neck.

I let the phone go as it dangled by the cord. My hands went to my neck and I dropped to my knees. Then I turned and sat on the curb. I couldn't breathe! I couldn't think! I looked up and all around me and I couldn't recognize anything!

Where on earth was I? I was beginning to hyperventilate. *What is happening to me?* I thought. *What happened?* I looked at my feet. I had no shoes on! I looked at my arms. They were so thin and long. That confused me, as I couldn't even remember who I was! I couldn't remember where I was or how I got there.

I heard a voice. It was a familiar voice. I was trying to place who sounded like that. I had never heard that voice so concerned before. I turned toward it and saw it was coming from the phone, and then I began remembering.

With what seemed like slow motion to me, I turned, stood up and reached with that foreign arm and pressed the phone against my ear. "Yes?"

Sue Ellen was hysterical. "Tammie!! My God! Where did you go? What is wrong with you!?"

"*Tammie?*" Yes. Okay, it started coming back into view. I started thinking, and I wanted to cry, remembering segments of those most recent events. His parents had to love me, for they had been in my life for twelve long years.

I didn't cry, but I began spilling my guts to this self-absorbed mother of his. "He's fine! I'm not! He did a terrible thing to me!"

Kevin's mother asked, "Tammie, what is it? What are you saying to me?"

I thought, "oh she does care! Finally, someone who cares!" I felt a warm current of fluid circulating through me.

Without a shred of shame for confiding in his parents, I advanced. "He went over the border and married this Mexican woman who showed up at my door *pregnant!* He left me at the house for weeks all *alone*, while she had the baby. He brought her and the baby back over to our home and then took them back, but *left* me *without* water and food for—"

Kevin's mother. Yeah, she was a real winner, that woman! She started yelping rudely in the background. "Oh wow!" We have a Mexican grandbaby? Did you hear that Robert, Kevin went out and got—"

I hung up on her. I felt sick and weak. I was terribly heartbroken over having been unloved for so long. Had I ever been comforted? I remembered laying my head down on Momma's lap while she stroked my hair with her hand. I must have been around eleven years old at that time. That only brought pain to my otherwise small life. Where had my family gone? Didn't anyone love me enough to come and find me? How could I have existed without love for all this time? How could it be that no one ever knew me? Did they just write me off? Did they forget me?

I sat back down on my defeated curb, put my hands over my face and began crying, very softy at first. The more tears that fell, the more came crashing through! I began crying louder.

I hadn't even realized that I was at a restaurant on the outskirts of the other side of town. I had never been inside. I had only seen it in passing when we drove to Kevin's twenty acres of desert property.

I thought, *what am I to do?* Then I got up and for the first time I called Momma collect. Momma told me that she would set it all up with my cousin in Dallas. She also told me that I would first have to get a car and money from Kevin. I was becoming nauseated at the idea of confronting Kevin for money and a car. I barely heard Momma's voice as she attempted to assure me that everything would be alright and that I shouldn't worry. When I got off the phone I was too confused to care much about anything. I still had no real resolution to work with. I began getting that feeling of displacement again. The road in front of me was so unfamiliar that I didn't know where I was. Where was I to go from there? I tried so hard to hold it together while my mind was still desperately searching for answers. All I knew was that I couldn't go back. Not now, at least. Maybe never. How could I face that beast again and safely get away? I had feared for my life! He had given me plenty of reason to.

Yet, my mother was correct in that I'd have no choice but to return to those battlegrounds once again. Alone. And there was a chance that he'd try, once again, to kill me. I trembled at the thought! It was a long way back to where I first started: my home was 1500 miles away. He owed that to me. I considered once again, the possibly fatal element attached to such a decision. It was something I would need time to work myself up to. Just the memory of his venom bit into my open wounds, making it difficult to even breath.

"Oh God, please, I am at the bottom of the well with no way to climb up for safety. Please Father, I ask for Your strength." I prayed inside myself for resolve, for direction, for love, for support, to just find a comfort in my brokenness.

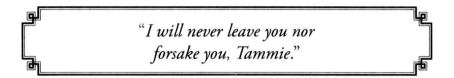

"I will never leave you nor
forsake you, Tammie."

I could hear these words like a warm rain pouring over my abandoned soul. I felt so small compared to the echo of the voice speaking mountains inside my head.

Leaving for home was a lot more than a simple drive out of town. I had to become a real-time warrior. All I wanted to do was lay down on the dusty caliche ground and become part of the earth itself, never to re-surface ever again! It felt like it would take a miracle to pull me from this dungeon of weighted chains. Yet, I knew that I had already broken loose. I just wasn't ready to face him again. At least not yet...

Maybe never...

CHAPTER TWENTY-EIGHT

Walking That Road of Darkness

1989 (27 Years Old)

My world was in ruin. I looked down at my feet again. Had I just walked across miles of desert terrain barefoot? *Where are you God? I need you so much.*

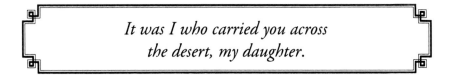

> *It was I who carried you across the desert, my daughter.*

All I could think was how very sad and perilous my life was at that moment. I had every intention of moving and getting up. I wanted to leave my spot on the concrete walkway next to the phone booth. I was falling into a pit of darkness. My life was meaningless.

What now? Where do I go from here? I thought to myself. *To what?*

My eyes looked down again toward the ground and, with shoulders slumped, I thought, *he has succeeded in proving I'm nobody's anything.*

It seemed I'd existed for all those years just to feed the beast.

I had forfeited my youth for an unknown purpose. Why was I not able to see through Kevin before? How could I have been blinded for so very long? I had lived under an umbrella of fear!

I looked at the ground between the faint image of my dirty feet. I was all that I had. I began crying a deep, defeated cry. It was the very cry Kevin had never allowed me to cry. All I heard were his mother's excited words about "the new grandbaby and daughter-in-law." I felt she intentionally avoided asking me if I was okay. That memory alone, drove a fresh new dagger into the soft part of my heart, twisting the sharpened edge over and again. Not even a hint of empathy over what had just devastated my existence. I felt like there was a red-hot steel rod down the center of my throat, through my chest, and into my stomach. There were waves of pain and then I began wailing, like some lone wolf, howling in the night. I thought, *breathe.*

I'd phoned my mother, who was concerned enough and had even planned for me to stay with a cousin. That would be a twelve-hour drive. I had no money. I seriously doubted that Kevin would give up a car and finance my trip home. I didn't know how to get home. I would be forever stuck, just as he warned me I would be. "You will never be anything without me!"

I began wailing again. Maybe if I laid down in the desert I could just shrivel up and let the winds blow my ashes up into the canyons. I felt striped, my head practically touching the ground in my despair. A woman couldn't possibly feel any lower.

No longer having him to protect me, I now had to protect myself against a world I knew nothing about. I reflected, *really, haven't I always been my own protector anyway?* I survived all those times alone in the desert with gun by my side. He tortured my soul and beat me blue. Still, why did I stay so long? He had forced me into staying all those years. Hadn't he? I no longer had the strength to carry myself home to Florida. How did I get this low?

Please, God, where are you?

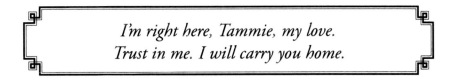

I'm right here, Tammie, my love.
Trust in me. I will carry you home.

A man approached me from the side. I wasn't even sure if he'd just walked up or had been standing there, watching the poor woman-girl cry. "Miss, are you okay?" His voice seemed so caring and soothing to my ears. I never got to hear that type of compassion. I yearned for the sound of my parents' voices or a sibling's laughter.

I looked up, battered and bewildered. Who was this man who stood above me?

"Please, won't you come inside the restaurant and have something to drink or eat?" I looked deeply into his eyes. Why was he bothering to care? But I reached up with my thin arm, taking the offered hand. Moving robotically, I allowed myself to be led into the empty restaurant. It was closing time.

He guided me to a booth. As I sat down, the man said, "Senorita, order anything you want." He was a big man, of Spanish decent with a Mexican accent and broken English. He stood looking down at me with a woman who he introduced as his wife.

"Okay. Thank you. Soup. Chicken noodle soup, please." I answered as best I could, as my weakened body on its last drop of adrenaline. The wife disappeared into the kitchen.

The man sat down across from me and for a split-second I wondered, *what is he expecting to happen here?* He must've read my surge of fear as he began to speak. "You seemed very upset sitting out there. You look very pale and, well, you just don't look too good, Senorita. Honestly, you look like a starved person from the desert lands. I just thought maybe some food would help you." The man gestured with his hands while he talked, which I thought seemed strange for a man. "My wife and I own this place. Are you out walking or did you drive here?"

I just sat there. I felt nothing, I said nothing. My eyes were swollen from crying. The clothes I had on were torn from the altercation with Kevin. I had thrown them on at some point the day before, or the day before that. Frankly I couldn't remember when I last took a shower. My hair was long past my shoulders. I had not brushed it for days, perhaps weeks.

The wife appeared from the kitchen with my steaming bowl of soup. I reached forward to accept it and saw my own arms that seemed to be detached from my body. I must've lost so much weight for lack of appetite over the past weeks. *As weak and fragile as I am*, I thought, *I must've been running on pure adrenaline when Kevin showed up at the house.*

I lost track of my own self. My mind began floating back to the house on the hill. I began thinking, *what happens when you lose something and someone that was never yours to begin with? Why doesn't anything make sense? Wasn't I ever woman enough? Nice enough? Didn't I work hard enough for him?* Nothing made any sense to me anymore. Not that it ever really did, now that I was forced to think about it.

The man lowered his voice, "Senorita, aren't you the girl that lives on the other side of town, on that hill?"

"No, I just don't know…" I said. I placed my hands over my ears, closed my eyes tightly and I felt Kevin's shards of glassy words pierce my skin over and over. The memory was so real to me of Kevin beating me on the head. His long fingers wrapped around my neck and began choking me. I could feel the world fading. I couldn't hold on to reality. I was so tired and worn out. I couldn't shake the feeling of my throat giving way under his fingers.

"Senorita, are you in any trouble? How can we help?" I opened my mouth to speak, without really knowing what to say. "My name is Tammie." I paused, searching for words. "I can't go home tonight. Please, can you take me home with you?"

It was a humiliating situation. I felt that a higher power was guiding me. *Don't question the sanity of it*, I told myself. Soon I would have no choice left but to return to that house on the hill when I felt it was safe enough. Kevin was my only way out. I still had to slay that dragon and then I'd be freed, forever. Until then, I had to submit to the whispering guidance.

The wife prompted me to eat and I obeyed. I ate as though I hadn't eaten in weeks, and was given another bowlful which I also devoured! All that time that Kevin was gone, I had been rationing the last bit of food that was there at the house. The soup was good for the stomach, but it was also feeding my brain. I started remembering everything all over again and I could no longer hold myself upright. Slumping over with a full napkin over my face, I once again began wailing like a wild abandoned wolf in the desert! I heard the foreign pitch in my voice and I wondered, *where did my body find this sound, this cry?* I had already fallen into the dark pits of hell. I'd never sounded so defeated in my life! I had never felt so lost and all alone. I had felt close to it, just never with this finality! The woman came and sat next to me, and wrapped me in her arms. She began stroking my hair like my momma used to do. She shushed me, saying that everything will be okay.

It was a good thing the restaurant was empty, for I held nothing back, pouring out my soul by the bucket loads. I was a faucet that couldn't be turned off. The woman leaned back a moment and handed me a pill with a glass of water insistently. "You need more relax," she said in her broken English.

> "Trust in the Lord with all your heart,
> and lean not on your own understanding."
> Proverbs 3:5

After I swallowed the pill with the glass of fresh, cool water, she again held me to console me. I just needed to cry it all out. I had not anyone else in the world to turn to. It wasn't that all my bridges were burned, I simply had no bridges in the first place. I fell into the love of that stranger's arms.

They took me to their home in Mexico that night. As we crossed the international bridge at the border, I knew that I was placing tremendous trust in these people. But I felt that God was guiding me, and through His mercy and grace, *I would be okay*. My broken soul felt affirmed.

CHAPTER TWENTY-NINE

Mexican Pharmacist

1989 (27 Years Old)

Throughout my journeys across Mexico, including trips to Torreón, Monterey, Durango, Mazatlán, El Paso, Del Rio, and Nuevo Laredo, I had never been to a Mexican family's home. I had always wanted to know more about the Mexican culture. Kevin was no longer there to censor my interactions, and I hoped I could learn more about their way of life. Would my retreat help me regain the strength needed to return to battle that dragon?

The restaurant owner and his wife formally introduced themselves once we reached their home. Before that moment, introductions seemed a lower priority than calming my broken soul. I sat there, in their kitchen, being treated like one of their own family members. I was finally beginning to focus, as the pill wore off.

"My name is Enrique, and this is my wife, Josefina. Welcome to our home," the man said. "You need something, tell me."

Just then, there was a knock on the door. Enrique had already told me that his niece was about to deliver a baby, and that his wife was a midwife. His niece would be delivering her baby at their house and there she was, ready to give birth.

I immediately recognized her face. It was my pharmacist, Yolanda! How did this happen? Enrique and Josefina were her aunt and uncle! I thought how odd that was!

Yolanda was screaming from the pain. Josefina motioned for them to go to one of the back rooms while Enrique and I stayed seated at the big kitchen table. But first she gave me a freshly-made tortilla with a plate of rice and beans, along with a big warm reassuring smile in her eyes. Again, I ate enthusiastically, and it felt so good to my stomach. Josefina then left for her screaming patient. Soon Enrique stood up and motioned for me to follow him.

As we rounded the corner of the bedroom door, I noticed how many relatives had come in the back door and were all gathered around. There was quite the audience of brothers, sisters, cousins, aunts, uncles, and friends. They all came and went as if it were just one big party. I saw Yolanda laying on the bed. Her skirt was pulled back as the aunt was trying to calm the new mother-to-be. I tried to act like I saw things like this all the time.

The truth was, I'd never seen a woman in labor, and especially never seen anyone in so much pain.

I looked around at all the loving family and friends who were there just for her. Yolanda was curled up, grasping her knees, pulling them back toward her chest, while trying to push her insides out, and screaming from the intense pain of the contractions.

It was all more than I could handle. I backed out of the room, walked down the hallway, and found a bedroom. It was so incredibly peaceful and inviting, I thought I'd lay down only for a quick nap. I was so exhausted. All the food that I had consumed in the past few hours was more than I'd consumed in a month. It only took a few seconds before I fell into a deep slumber.

I woke up hot, with sweat lining my upper lip and my clothes damp. My initial thought was *where on earth am I?* Then I remembered and thought, *wow it is really hot! Why isn't their AC on?* As I got up, I realized they had no AC. That was their life. I was in Mexico.

I wondered how long I had been sleeping. It was still dark out, but I could hear the birds chirping outside the open window and I believed it was morning time. Sometime during the night someone had come in to lay a sheet over me. I scoped out the room. I remembered the bedroom I'd been in at Kevin's parents' and grandparents' houses. I hadn't seen many finished rooms like that since I was fifteen years old, living at home with my parents.

This room was simple in the Spanish décor and it exuded the love of a family. How could it be that I lived for all those years without love? I started getting the tight knot again and the scalding rod down my center. In the past I never let myself feel such things like sorrow, intense pain, or depression. I'd always kept them out of my reach for fear of drowning in them. This time was different though. No more protective shield or bubble. Kevin had bursts all hope I had left in this world.

I sat on the edge of the bed and felt sorrow for what I had needed for all those years of my life growing up: love. Plain, simple love. I began softly crying for a love that I wasn't even sure I'd ever obtain. There, inside those strangers' house, in another country, without a person in the world knowing where I was, I softly cried for me. I had felt more love from those strangers in a day than I had for over a decade. How could this be? Didn't I deserve love?

Then it hit me! What was I doing? Where was I? I sprang to the open window to see something familiar. Anything. If I decided to leave this house and begin walking I had absolutely no idea in which direction I should take to get back over the international border to the US.

I was broken, panic-stricken, and emotionally drained. I turned around and retreated to my seat on the edge of that bed. Elbows on knees, I covered my face with my hands and cried even more. I figured I must be crying all the tears that had been on reserve for all those past years.

Kevin had never let me cry. He would scold me about how only low-life's cried. People with dignity didn't. Yet, because of him I forever had tears lingering on the edge of my prisoned mind. It was all so very overwhelming for me and I was exhausted. I lay back down across the bed. *Just sleep.*

I loved these people and their beautiful hearts! I wanted nothing more than to bask in their loving environment, but I knew it would be time to leave soon. I had a mission to complete. I needed to start on my eastward journey to a home that I left so many years before. I ached at the thought that I had never mattered to anyone.

Waking again from a deep and nourishing sleep, I scooted to the side of the bed. It was Yolanda who found me awake. She came in and sat next to me. She didn't look anything like someone who just gone through the labor of childbirth. But Yolanda told me that I had been there for 3 days. Josefina had instructed the family to not wake me up, that I needed rest.

She spoke to me in English, "I don't know what happened in your life, but I am no longer your pharmacist, I am your friend." She embraced me as the tears fell down my face. "I am here for you, to support you right now. So, lean on me. It's okay, I won't let you fall."

She sat there with me until my tears diminished. She told me that her Auntie Josefina was watching over her new baby girl. "Why don't I show you where the shower is? I gathered some things for you. It will make you feel better." I agreed after thanking her for being there for me and congratulating her on her new baby.

I followed Yolanda to the courtyard, at the center of the u-shaped house. There, across the dusty hardened earth, was a small adobe hut with a large round metal cistern sitting on top. Pipes extended out of its side and were pointing downwards to the flat top roof.

As we entered, she showed me the one showerhead on the side of the wall. "The water in the tub on the roof is already hot and there is a cold-water knob. Best to not take too long or you will only have cold left." She handed me a bar of soap, shampoo, lotion, washcloth, towel, flip flops, t-shirt, and a modest skirt.

She also gave me undergarments that were brand new with tags still on. She told me that she had just bought them from the store on the corner, "just for you." I was getting such special attention and I wondered why. Had God really appointed these people to care for me in my most desperate time of need?

Left to manage the shower on my own, I took charge. When I stood underneath that hot shower water I felt that I had now experienced a part of what heaven must really feel like. *Look! no hands!* I thought to myself. I'd spent all those years pouring my shower water from a green plastic gardening spout container.

I was in a good place! And I was grateful that I was in a real home on that day, so nothing else mattered to me! The shower made me feel fresh and alive. I picked up the clothes I had removed and noticed how light they were. I had done a number on them from years of washing on the scrub board. They were paper thin. The collar was ripped, and the sleeve cuff was half torn off from the struggle with Kevin. They were dingy and smelled bad too.

Yolanda had me to sit on the patio bench while she put conditioner in my hair and began combing out the knots. It took rinsing and reapplying more conditioner, for my hair was badly tangled. She then French braided my hair. I had an audience of 5 little girls watching.

Yolanda finished with my hair and we moved into the kitchen to have lunch. After eating more beans and rice with fresh tortillas and goat cheese, we left the kitchen for the living room. There were upright chairs waiting for us and the older folk were seated on the couch. They offered to get up, but I insisted that I sit in a chair. A relative began playing a guitar and singing mariachi style music. It was so surreal for me to sit still, trying not to be anything but engaged in the group. I was grateful and honored to be sharing their afternoon with them.

I loved the Mexican culture, the music, the language. Their eyes smiled before their mouths. There were bad people in all countries; that's just the way of the world. But I felt safe in Mexico. I always had. As I listened to the melodic rhythm of the guitarist, I thought of Kevin. As foreign as this land was to me, I had never been away from him before. Except of course, at the house on the hill, when he left me.

I felt an element of guilt, and an element of freedom. It was scary to feed either emotion, for my future was so unsure. My freedom had not yet been achieved. I still had dangerous roads to travel.

It was still very much a battle to overcome. The guilt came from being away from that man who was all I ever had. No matter how he had treated me, guilt was trying to plant fresh daggers in my gut. His words commanded my thoughts, "After all I've done for you...." Then I touched my throat after swallowing a ball of air that was lodged somewhere halfway down. *I had reason enough to leave, right?* I whispered in my thoughts. And with that, I tuned out my irrational fears and turned to the music that was played so passionately. It brought tears to my eyes.

I really tried to live inside that moment, but my worries kept crowding in. My mind was just so full of heaviness. I was getting more anxious about the trials in front of me. I wished that somehow, I could take all those people with me to protect me from his wrath. But it wasn't their battle. They did what they were called to do for me, and I will always be grateful. But I knew that I would never again see them. I would carry them inside my soul forever. My eyes moved from one person to the next. I tried to stamp their images into my memory, so I could replay this moment over and again. I promised myself I'd never forget what they did for me, and I'd always remember them with the endearing thoughts they so deserved.

They took a young American woman, all battered, broken, tattered, and torn, and drove her to their homeland. They opened their home to me and never asked for anything in return. They brought me back from a deep dark place that Kevin had shoved me into.

I hoped to recover from all this someday. In his cruelty, Kevin would want me to continue feeling badly about myself. Or perhaps sink to the bottom of some deep ocean, and drown. Or wither away and drink myself to death, to be blown away and scattered across the desert lands. He had conditioned me to not think, to not feel, and to not speak.

I was determined to prove his words and opinions wrong! I would go back to that house on that hill with my newfound strength and stand tall once more! I would stay only long enough to pack a car and leave. The car he would provide for me. And he would give me the funds it would take to survive the long haul through the desert! I was going home to Florida where I would reunite with my family.

But for now, I could not think past getting to that house and leaving. I just couldn't. The thought of it all made me shudder with fear and trigger my gag reflex.

✦

I must continue to be the warrior that God appointed me to be, I told myself as Yolanda drove me across the border and to the foot of the hill of Kevin's driveway. She pulled her small car with Mexican plates to a full stop. "Listen now, my friend, don't you ever forget me! Be strong, be true, be you! God specially made a way out for you! Go slay that dragon and be safe. You have God on your side, Tammie, there is no reason to be afraid anymore! Be done, my friend!" We hugged goodbye, with tears pouring down our faces, both knowing that we'd never see the other again. "Vaya con Dios! Tammie, I'll never forget you!"

Away Yolanda drove, and I turned around in slow motion and looked up that hill, with its rocky uneven terrain, leading to the house of my past horrors. Already, those experiences seemed so far away as though I'd somehow said my goodbyes before that moment.

Then, from the top of the hill, the blinding reflection of the sun glared into my eyes off the side-view mirror of his truck, as I saw Kevin spring the door open. And so, it began, the beginning of the end…

CHAPTER THIRTY

※ ◆ ※

The Open Road

1989 (27 Years Old)

"So, you've decided to come back! What have I told you about leaving? I said…"

"I am not here to stay." I interrupted. "I don't want any trouble with you. I am leaving, and I need you to help me. I have nothing to my name but my few clothes." I was nervous, but attempted to hide my fear.

Kevin crossed his arms. "Uh, huh… You think I'm going to help you? I have already told you if you leave you will do it on your own! You have cost me too much money to give you anything more."

A stiffness was growing in my throat and the top half of my head was already getting warm. I had already known that the only car available for him to turn over to me would've been my Mustang. I knew that he wasn't about to let me leave with that car. No matter how many times he boasted about it being *my* car (a gift for all the abuse), he was a swindler. There wasn't an honest bone in that man's body.

"Kevin, I need a car and I need money to leave with."

But Kevin had evidently already planned for this. Sitting on that hill was an old Toyota that I'd not seen before. Kevin gestured toward the vehicle. "You can have Tatiana's car! It's gassed up and ready for you."

I thought if he said one more word to me with her name attached to it, I would end up picking something up and throwing it at him. I still wasn't over the trauma of recent events and my wounds of rejection were still very fresh. "Fine!"

Kevin's next words hit hard. "You need to hurry. She will be home soon with the baby. She's coming over with her friends to decorate her new house."

My stomach gurgled and churned with that putrid coating, and I just knew I would get sick. I held back the urge and beefed up my courage. It was the only thing holding me upright at that moment. I began gathering all my things that I had previously boxed up. There was enough to fill the back seat and the passenger seat of the little car. I tried to block out all that he was saying to me somewhere in the background. I couldn't look at him or speak to him. I simply ignored him.

"You know I love you Tammie, I have always been good to you. We have shared love for many years. We have had some good times too. It's not too late to change your mind! Why don't you just come back inside and stay. We can all work this out." He got more desperate the longer he talked.

I was hurrying at this point, working as fast as I could. I was focused on the driveway and driving down it for the last time! "I am ready to go now Kevin, I need money to leave with." I knew this was the part where he could hold me back if he wanted to. I was totally dependent on his handout and he knew that! I had promised myself to not give in, no matter what he gave me. I would say nothing.

Not even goodbye.

"Now, I am on disability, Tammie, so I don't have much money to give you. I hadn't planned on this expense. I'm just a poor man and you know that about me." He said.

I knew he was so full of crap! He had money enough to hold down two houses, one in Texas and one across the border with his wife! But I let him play his little game as I stood emotionless, expressionless. I knew this was the last game he would ever be able to play with me. When I drove down that driveway I would never turn around nor ever bow down to this man ever again! I would prove wrong every single lie he ever put in my head! I thought, *you're an A1 authentic pompous ass!* Which made me smirk, thinking of his ears growing tall and his teeth becoming bucked like a donkey's. *That Mexican woman can have him! I'm done with his nothingness!*

He was playing like the money issue was going to break his bank wide open! "I don't know, Tammie. How much do you think you will need?"

I realized he was giving me a car with a history unknown to us both. And money? I had heard him cry the woes to his grandparents before when they needed something from him. I responded sarcastically with, "Well Kevin, I will be traveling 1,500 miles to get to back home. What do you think?" Honestly, I had not been prepared for that question and had no clue about how much things cost.

"Okay, well, I can't give you much, Tammie. Here take this. That should get you there."

I stood there looking at the money, knowing it was not enough! It was a hundred-dollar bill and five ones. But my pride would not allow me to defend myself to this butt-faced man.

"Kevin, I will take the money, but I need to ask for one thing that you have that belongs to me."

"Yeah? And what would that be?" He asked with sudden irritation, as his hands flew to his hips.

I swallowed hard. "You took naked pictures of me when I was just fourteen years old. I would like you to give them to me!"

He laughed as though what I said was trivial and not interesting to him at all, "Oh, those pictures? Those are with my collection. They belong with my other girls! They're not yours to have!" Those were his exact words.

I felt a storm building. My throat was getting tight, my hands began itching as they closed into fists. I was woman now! I laid claim to my own value at that moment. I turned on my heel and walked around his wife's stupid little car to the driver's door. I opened that door, got in, turned the car over, and didn't even wait for it to warm up. I needed to go in *Planck time*! I would be much happier if I were in a rocket, but I guessed that his *wife's* car would have to work!

I did not allow myself to look back. I stared forward as though I would be struck with lightning, or turned to salt if I turned around to see him smiling.

There were three main roads that lead out of town. My Mexican friends had told me which one to take. As I drove up and over the climb of the road and around the bend, the town fell out of sight. That is when I looked in the rearview mirror.

I began crying from all the dreams that had shattered in my life through my 27th year. I mourned for everything I had lost. I cried out loud. Really loud!

There was no one for many miles away, no one could hear me, and no one could see me. No one could feel me. No one knew me. No one could find me if something were to happen to me.

I cried for all the reasons I was leaving. I was so full of anger, yet I was so full of love for a land I never wanted to forget. I grieved for my desert, as though it were somehow my father. Kevin had crushed my dreams and stole my innocence away, yet as I trembled in the face of my aloneness I realized *I was still me.*

He did not have the power to make me dissolve. Through all the physical abuse and the continuously scornful insults and humiliations, my own strength still protected me. God still protected me.

Had I always been this strong? I silently reflected, *I have proven to myself that I am willing to fight and to slay the dragons to escape such dungeons. I will not be overcome ever again. I am a warrior.*

I vowed on that day to protect myself from any Kevins I ever encountered again! My life was going to be filled with so many new adventures! I just knew that life would never be the same as the one I had just left.

♦

She's Gone

Wondering off in the open plain,
Winds blowing past with distant light rain.
Never to worry with such things up ahead,
"I will fight for you, die for you," is what he had said.
To offer a life so far away from my scars,
To the land of no trees, no people, just stars.
He lowered me down into that deep open well.
Where scorpions and snakes so frequently fell.
Full moon, full moon, looking down on me,
Shine your moonlight on that forbidden key,
Sage and white rock and cacti at ground level,
Rainbows from stained glass and diamond-shaped bevel.
Inside the mirror what more can there be,
But that Spanish woman's voice, where once there was me.

CHAPTER THIRTY-ONE

So Far Away

1989 (27 Years Old)

The desert was a lonely road. It was the same landscape for miles, the same color of sand and boulders. The same view in all directions. I wanted to call my family but there were no pay phones. There weren't even any towns, unless dried up, unoccupied ghost towns counted. I was holding onto a bigger thread of hope than I had. It was hot, but I didn't want to use the car's air conditioner. I was afraid of something happening to a car that I knew nothing about.

I desperately wanted to hear something on the radio but there weren't any towers to broadcast radio stations where I was. This was a strip of road in the desert with no signs of life. I had been driving for hours and not one car had passed me on the road.

I was distraught. I desperately wanted to fast forward to my arrival. It was spooky driving in the no man's land. Alone. I didn't even see a police car. This route would get me to my cousin's house in Dallas. That was a twelve-hour drive. My friends in Mexico had told me which road to take to get me there. I trusted them, but I wanted a map to see for myself. From Dallas I would take a bus to Florida.

Thinking about my recent experience in Mexico, I was incredibly humbled by those peoples' hospitality. Kevin had abused me for so many years that I didn't even understand the extent of it. I still thought that some of it was quite normal. Yolanda helped to clarify that for me, though. She had said that none of the abuse was normal. She affirmed that nothing was my fault and that I never deserved to be his victim.

I reflected what my friend said to me before we parted: "Tammie, you needed to leave him! It is not right what he has done to you all these years! You do have other options. You can become anything you want!"

"It's just that I am so afraid of failing," I confided to her.

"That depends on your own actions. You can do whatever you want with your life. To do nothing and fail or take control and succeed!" She was busy rolling the flour out to make a fresh batch of tortillas. "It's your life now. I am so proud of you and what you have done so far! You've broken through barriers." She poured water into a pot of beans, then turned up the flame. She turned to me with such sincerity. "You took the first step already, lady, and you can't stop now! Keep taking those first steps as you move forward!"

"I will! You have given me so much support, my friend! I'm only sorry that we won't see each other ever again. Your family has done so much for me, how could I ever repay you?" It made me sad to leave and I told her so. I had finally made a friend and now I had to leave her.

I had contemplated staying in Mexico and taking them on as my new family. It was already proven that I could live the simpler life, but I also wanted to get back to my own family again. I had to choose.

Yolanda hugged me. "You have already paid us back, Tammie, just by letting us guide you toward your home and the family who loves you. That is enough payment. Just follow through. Follow your dreams! Don't let anything or anyone ever stand in your way! You are so far away from the east coast. There's a long journey ahead of you, my friend."

Just then the car shuddered and died, shocking me out of my reverie. It was so quiet without the rumble of the engine. All I could hear were the tires crunching on the sandy pavement as it coasted to a stop!

I tried turning it over and there was nothing but silence. I looked in my rearview mirror at emptiness behind me and emptiness through the windshield in front of me. I got out of the car and began crying again. I started yelling at God, shaking both hands up at the sky as I began trembling all over. I was falling apart, as I fell to my knees.

"What now God? I don't even have a gun! No protection! Nothing! I am exposed and at Your mercy! I just don't want to do this anymore! I won't go back! I am in the middle of the desert and I don't even have supplies with me to survive! Why? Why is this happening to me God? Someone could kill me, and no one would ever hear me scream! Please God, help me!"

> *Say to those with fearful hearts,*
> *"Be strong, do not fear, your God will come,*
> *He will come with vengeance, with divine*
> *retribution, He will come to save you."*
> Isaiah 35:4

Just then my worst nightmare unfolded before my eyes! I got up from my knees and stared in the distance. There on the horizon as the heat danced just above the level of the road, I saw it taking form. It was still far away, but I could tell it was a vehicle. I was terrified!

"So, this is it God? This is how I will die? Out in the middle of the desert, God? Really? Please God, don't let me suffer! Please God, I have suffered most of my life, God! Please spare me this!" I was begging for my life, watching the dancing wave bring a white dot closer. "I promise I will be good! I promise you, God, I will do good things! Please promise me safety through my life! Please don't let me die like this, God!"

The dot morphed into an old white Cadillac. I didn't even get back inside the car! I just stood there. I was fully convinced I was going to die and I wanted to let that driver know I was wide awake and aware of my own environment! I would not go easily.

He slowed down and stopped next to me. I could see what he looked like. My fears were confirmed. His hair was long and fluffy in the back and bushy and wiry all over his face.

"Oh God, this is it! Please, I beg, don't let me suffer, God!"

The hairy man spoke. "How d' ya do, Ma'am?"

My mouth had to be forced to move. "Okay, except that my car stopped working."

The man kindly asked, "you mind if I take a look? I'm pretty good with engines and things."

Standing there in a stupor I answered, "No, please."

He pulled over behind my car and came up to the driver's door, opened it, got on his knees, and looked under the dash beneath the steering wheel. He pulled something out and went to his car, returning with some tools.

"Let's pray it's this simple," he smiled.

I thought, "so, the man prays! Maybe he's just trying to impress me!"

He turned the engine over and the stupid car started right up for him!

"A water pump fuse! That's all it was! It was a wild guess, but the first thing I thought to check."

"You are kidding me! That's it!" My shoulders relaxed, and I trembled with relief that he was able to repair the car, and so quickly! "Well, thank you so much, Sir, I don't have much money, but I could give you two dollars for the fuse."

"Oh no! Please, it was nothing! Where are you headed to?"

"Um, a couple of more towns over, going to my aunt's house."

The hairy man responded, "well, are you hungry? My place is just down the road a bit. I would be obliged if you let me make us some dinner."

"Oh, well, um, look. I really appreciate what you've done, but my family is waiting for me. I'm sorry but I must go now. Thank you again for fixing my car, I am most grateful!"

He said goodbye, and he sadly went on his way. I thought the poor man must be lonely! Nonetheless, I wasn't going to do something so asinine as to follow a stranger home!

I took a very important moment out in my most precious life. As I sat with both hands on the wheel on the side of that deserted desert road, and I said a prayer of thanks to God for saving my life. He didn't send me anything but an angel to fix my car!

I arrived in Dallas just before nightfall. But the car stalled out on me again twenty-five miles from my cousin's house! I was able to find a payphone and asked her to come pick me up. What a nice way to arrive to someone's house. *Needy!* I thought. *Yay for me*, I had made such a wonderful first impression in this new life! Yet my cousin Beverly was very kind to come pick me up.

I stayed in Dallas for a few weeks, working at Belgian's Restaurant, waiting tables. I didn't talk to anyone about the trauma I had just escaped from. I was anxious to get back to the east coast, putting as many miles between me and Kevin as possible. Besides, I never wanted to impose on Beverly's most charming hospitality. I loved her so much and it was nice to be with family again. Within the first week I had made enough money to ship my stuff to my parents' house in Florida.

After a week and a half more, I had saved up the rest of the money I needed to leave for Florida. I bought a bus ticket for the east coast, and was so eager to get back home that I boarded that bus very sick with a bad cold. I asked the driver how many buses it would take to get there. He informed me that he would be the only driver and that was his bus. I was fortunate to get a front row seat and asked if he could watch over me, that I needed to take Robitussin but that I knew it would knock me out.

"Sure thing, Miss! You just lay right there across those seats and don't you worry about a thing! I'm not going to let anything happen to you!" He announced.

I was so happy to hear that, and I fell fast asleep for most of my nine-hundred-mile journey.

The bus driver woke me once. "Miss, you might want to get up and at least go in that gift store and buy yourself a t-shirt, saying that you was in New Orleans! I'll be right here! Your things won't be touched. I'll watch over them for you!"

"Oh, thank you, sir! I think I will!" As I stretched I noticed how dizzy I felt from the medicine, but was thrilled once I went into the store and bought myself a royal blue Mardi Gras shirt! I loved it!

The next morning my daddy picked me up from the bus station and we went to my parents' house. I felt a ball in the pit of my stomach when I got there and realized that I was in my hometown, jobless and broke!

My younger brother, Ben, was now 17 and we were so excited to spend some time together. My mom and dad were quite the pair. I am not sure why they had trouble with their marriage throughout the years, but by the time I moved back from Texas, they had been divorced from each other a total of three times. The joy of the confusion is that they still loved one another. Some say it was their way of keeping their marriage interesting and exciting. They still desired to be married. Hence, they had their fourth marriage arranged as a wedding in the church, inviting all five of their children to participate. I had made it home in time to be part of the wedding.

That was only the second wedding I'd ever seen in person.

I was thrilled to spend quality time with my family. It had been so long. I hadn't spent this much time around anyone other than Kevin in over a decade, except for Beverly in Dallas.

I wasn't quite sure where I fit in this world. I knew that I needed to go away once more to find what was missing inside of me.

People wanted to know things that I didn't want to talk about. I just needed to get away and regroup from my long journey east.

PROLOGUE CONTINUED:
PUTTING IT ALL BEHIND ME

Riding south to Key West with Caroline, my sister, and her husband, Henry, was an opportunity from Heaven. I was feeling emotional and overwhelmed with learning how to socialize again. I had spent so much time in solitude. I didn't wish to stick out in the crowd. I wanted to be treated as normal. I knew that I had a problem with things triggering memories from my past. I had terrible flashbacks of abuse and unworthiness.

There was no other way to move except forward. I was exposed to a world too large to digest that frequently left me exhausted and weak. Somehow, I was both too young to know any better, and too old to be so naïve. The world was not my own. My own foundation had been ripped out from under me and I could not understand the new one that other people assumed for me. I had to relearn how to dissect the good parts from the bad. I felt exposed and disoriented, and I didn't know where to begin.

I couldn't possibly tell anyone what I'd just come from. A moment of being misrepresented and surely misunderstood would knock my heart right out of my chest once again. No one knew me. No one would know me for years to come. I promised myself that I would not talk about Kevin and what he did to me and what he made me live through! All I wanted was to forget!

God had saved my life for a purpose unknown to me.

CHAPTER THIRTY-TWO

Opened Doors, As He Promised

1990 (27 Years Old)

My True Love Has Arrived

My birth came to pass, with pink ribbons and lace.
My legs, they grew longer, from wobble to grace.
The pearls in my eyes reflect the color of light,
Kaleidoscope motion, with such meaning in sight.
My hands were the backdrop, to wipe away tears,
My heart was the portal, for dreams without fears.
Away getting prepped, by the hands of His grace,
Was glory and marvel, moving on with the race.
His body is strong, his voice is not wrong,
For God wants him toned, to sing me his love song.
He was made apart from my life, to compliment what mine is,
I am his love, to receive all his gifts.
God has the wings, for the angels to guide,
Once all is complete,

My true love will arrive...

♦

I turned 17 when I was 27. Having left all society at the young age of 15 and always being entirely dependent on someone else had left me without a clue as to how to be an adult. How was I to go into the civilized world and not stick out? I didn't really know about the outside world. But really, it wasn't the outside world that concerned me so much as my internal battle. I feared that battle would leave me vulnerable. I also feared it would take years, if not decades, for me to catch up with my age and to appear normal to others.

But I ended up living in the most amazing place with sister, Caroline, and brother-in-law, Henry! Key West was even better than I imagined. When we arrived, they took me on my first drive down Duval Street. It wasn't even real to me. From the backseat of their white Bronco I sat in a stupor. While Caroline and Henry were in the front seats, chatting away, probably even to me, my mind was overwhelmed by the flood of visual information!

Same-sex couples walked down the street, hand in hand. I saw a man tattooed from his feet to his face, and a man riding a motorcycle with his poodle, groomed with a green mohawk, riding on the tank in front of him. Groups of people came out of one bar and entered another. I was told they were doing the "Duval crawl."

I wondered how far this island's reality was from real life. Somehow, I wasn't afraid of being wrongly influenced but I had so much to learn. *How*, I thought, *can I possibly learn everything in the flash of a moment?* I had lost so much time. I was breathless, thinking of how there was so much in life to explore! I was so excited to get started!

I immediately got a waitress job and signed up for certified nursing assistant classes at the adult learning center, as well as a book-keeping/accounting class. I had no clue what my interest would be; all that I wanted was to find my independence. That way I'd never be dependent again on anyone. That way I would prove Kevin wrong. I was not going to fail!

The more water that separated me from the mainland, the more content I was! That place would be my island for healing and renewal. I could only take America a little at a time. I had a lot to learn and this was not going to be easy. Just how difficult would it prove to be, only time would reveal.

I was living on a houseboat with Caroline and Henry. I slept in the bow of the boat. It was a most glorious introduction back into civilization. I would rise early in the morning and, even before coffee, I would don my new bathing suit and slip into the crystal-clear water at the stern of the boat! This was my favorite thing to do! It had a calming effect on my soul.

My soul needed calming. The nightmares continued, and I would stay on the island until I felt stronger to face the world.

Eventually, I gave in to Henry and his desires to marry me off to a *good and decent man*. I went on a few dates that he set me up with. The first was with a man who could have been Brad Pitt's twin. Of course, I had no clue who Mr. Pitt was at that time. I only knew the guy in question was dreamy looking. After dinner, we kissed, one simple kiss. I backed away as we looked deeply into one another's eyes, but not dreamily. No, it was more in confusion. It felt like I had just kissed a dry sponge. Like it'd feel if someone kissed their brother! Ewww! We agreed that neither of us got anything from that kiss. In hindsight, that was the beginning of my journey into adulthood.

I didn't want to believe that the reaction to that one kiss was because I had no love inside of me to feel. My brother-in-law set me up with two more dates, but both were disasters! The dinners were exquisite, and the guys were handsome enough and well-educated. But they each approached me after dinner as though I was supposed to have sex with them! They acted like it was the norm! *What was with these guys!*

I told Henry that the social norms were wrong! No more dates! It made me realize I had no intentions of dating for a long time, *if ever*! No, thank you, I did not need to be *hooked up* with anyone.

Key West was a physically active place where I learned to be young. I could not have been brought to a more desirable place! I enjoyed water skiing behind Henry and Caroline's boat, jet-skiing, snorkeling, cycling the island, and playing volleyball on the beach. I ended up winning Australian surfboard contests! It was awesome playing limbo and other beach games when the spring breakers came down from Miami! The world, as I was experiencing it, had taken on a new meaning. I was incredibly excited from the moment I opened my eyes in the morning until I closed them for sleep. I was excited the whole time that I lived on that island!

The energy surrounding the many people on vacation was inspiring and invigorating! That time of coming to myself and learning about people and a different environment was the most amazing experience of my life up to that point! I constantly had goosebumps on my skin as my soul went into a feeding frenzy. My inner spirit soaked in the beauty of the walks down the tropical canopied paths. I wanted nothing less than to know and feel the essence of paradise in every inch of that newfound life. I walked for days and weeks. I would retire each night completely exhausted, only to set out exploring again the very next sunrise! There was so much to see. I enjoyed experiencing the architectural splendor of houses that weren't built of *adobe blocks*.

I lived at the marina on the military base which happened to have a sandy beach. There was a regular group that came there several times a week to play volleyball, my favorite sport! I would also go bowling with the same group. I became part of their crowd; it was Mat, Dennis, Michelle, Jill, and me. We were inseparable. They were enlisted and worked as military police. Even though they were all seven to eight years younger than me, they didn't notice one bit. I was as innocent as a baby bird, and they were just past their teens themselves. I went to the military gym with them, I went out to eat with them, and I observed their craziness at clubs. We had so much fun together! I thought I'd bust my stomach muscles for all the laughter. They never once judged me. They did wonder about me from time to time, as my life was not void of flashbacks.

Those were times when everything was going good and, out of nowhere, something would trigger a memory that would force me into reliving my past trauma. It could be anywhere, anytime. Any one person could innocently say something to me, and it would trigger a panic attack. It would throw me into my past. My heart would begin doing aerobics in my chest, and I wouldn't be able to breathe.

I would run for cover, sheltering myself from the perceived threat. I would just disappear, and stay gone.

One day, Jill asked me, "what happened to you, Tammie?"

I responded, "It's not anything. I deal with it. I just have my own way."

They learned that when I disappeared for days, it would be okay and eventually I'd be back. I had told them that I would never hold anything against them, that it was me who had the problem, not them.

That's how I had dealt with the abuse from Kevin all those years. He would embarrass me in front of his family by hitting me or degrading me with words, and I would remove myself from them, and inject my soul into the bubble that kept me safe from destruction.

Those memories, they crept into my veins, and any joy I was feeling prior to that moment, would abruptly fade away! It was difficult to make friends because of it. I couldn't allow others to see me that way. I felt ugly and somehow disfigured. I lived on the island for eight months. During that time, I began working as a bartender in training. I needed to save money since I had nothing to my name. I did the bartending for a couple of weeks before I realized that the bar life was not my cup of tea.

I had also applied for a waiter job at the restaurant next door. I received a call that I had the job! I was so happy to be free from the bartender position. Waitress work was so physically demanding, and I liked the challenge. I was accustomed to hard work.

Everything was a new experience to me. I was clueless but I was also a sponge, learning everything that came across my path! I was so determined! I could not fail. It was up to me to make my life work out! As long as no one looked too closely, they wouldn't know what I didn't know! They wouldn't see the cracks that were caused by all the years of being kept in seclusion.

I rented my own apartment where I practiced walking with a book on my head. I practiced painting my nails. I practiced speaking, by reading aloud enthusiastically. I took long walks through the neighborhoods, the marinas, and the main streets of Key West, marveling at how people appeared to be so well put together.

There were times when the pressures of the new and exciting world just became too much for me. I became exhaustingly over-whelmed. I frequently took a drive down Roosevelt Boulevard to a Catholic Church. Since all my visits there were during the daytime hours on a weekday, I had seen no one inside but the priest. He always stayed in the background until I was ready to leave. At the exit, he would be ready to bless me and give me a hug good-bye.

After entering the church, I'd select a random bench seat, pull down the kneeler in front of me, and kneel in prayer. Every time I went, I was in distress, almost to a breaking point. I revealed my opened wounds to God. As my soul bled out I cried aloud, pouring everything out to the cross, "*please help me, God. Help me find my way, help me to have more strength to overcome the ugly scars. Please take away my pain that tears at my soul. Please take away the memories. Please God, I beg of Your mercy to take this pain away.*" I'd cry and cry, hearing my words echo in the cathedral ceilings. I held nothing back! The spiritual presence of God held me tight and told me that I was worthy. He told me He brought me to that place to open the doors of opportunity for healing to begin. He told me that my life would someday be used as a testament to help others overcome oppression. He promised me that the open doors would reveal my path. He told me to practice patience and to give love to others who are broken like me.

Afterwards, I felt a sense of renewal. Every single time. God spoke to me repeatedly like mountains inside my mind. Just as He did when I lived in the desert. He covered me with a love that reassured my broken heart. He was there with me, and would never leave my side.

Still, without knowing more about God and walking in faith, I'd fall back into my broken self. I had built boundaries, keeping others from seeing *me*, preventing them from seeing my scars, from seeing how broken I was. I refused to be held down by the razor-sharp memories that slashed away at me. I kept moving forward as my internal pain continued.

God's love helped me to safely escape that valley on the western ridge of a Texan mountain range only months before. So, I never gave up hope.

I still hung out at my family's boathouse. I loved the volleyball games and my sister and brother-in-law showered me with much needed love! My skin had tanned to a rich tropical bronze, as I had allowed myself that privilege for the season. No one would ever tell me what I could or could not do with my body, ever again! But I would always wear a long t-shirt out on the beach area when sailors were around.

One beautiful day I was there on the white sandy beach next to the marina, waiting to play the next volleyball set. My team had already won, having already been playing there for hours that day. I was standing about three feet from the net pole, watching the game in play.

I knew there were sailors sitting nearby at the café cabana. They were part of the next team to play us. They were all being overzealous with their voices, and I could tell they weren't the usual guys stationed on that base but were visiting from another command.

I heard one of them say, as I stood with my back to them, "I wonder where she's from."

The other sailor said, "I don't know but I wonder what her name is."

Then another one said, "I wonder how old she is."

I was 28 but looked 18 since I had been kept away from all that would age me. This got my attention, as I knew someone was about to put their foot in their mouth!

"Oh, I don't know, maybe about 35!" was the exaggerated replay.

I turned around and knew without a doubt who had said that. I turned back around and decided to ignore them.

Then it was time for my team to play and I was so excited! I took my place at the net and the guy facing me from the other team, was HIM! The insulter!

He looked over the rim of his Ray-Ban Wayfarers with his over-confident smile and said, "may I ask you out for a date?"

I had to admit that he was tall and handsome. He had a cute cleft chin and, well, just an air about him I couldn't put my finger on. But I had my pride, and so I responded without hesitation. "No way!"

He said flirtatiously, "oh, you mean back there. I had to figure out a way to get your attention."

"Well, it worked, didn't it?" I snapped back.

"I really want to take you out for dinner and then maybe out to Margaritaville for a drink!" He persisted.

"No way!" I said again.

We kept playing volleyball. The conversation came in segments as we were being rotated for the serve.

"You'll have fun, come with me tonight!" He pressed.

Finally, I gave him what he wanted. "Fine, I'll go. Meet me tonight at five at the bar here on the base."

His eyebrows flew up with surprise as he said, "Really? Great! I'll meet you there at 5 o'clock!"

At 5:15 I called the bar. I spoke to the bartender, telling him my name and to let the Chevy Chase looking guy named Stephen know that I couldn't make it. I was feeling slightly guilty but continued bowling with my friends anyway. I didn't know what to say to him. I already had established friends. It took them a long time to learn and accept my quirks!

The next afternoon, which was a Saturday, I was on my sister's houseboat, microwaving a frozen lobster I'd taken from the freezer for my dinner. I was looking out the front window when I saw a new white Cadillac arrive at the pier! A guy got out all dressed in white with the deepest, darkest suntan I'd ever seen. He had on a white polo, with white shorts showing his long tan legs, and white tennis shoes. He headed down the pier towards us. I was in a daze about his dreamy look, and my sister spotted him too.

"Look, Tammie, he's so handsome!" She was always trying to hook me up with someone!

I immediately snapped out of my trance and gasped with recognition, "oh NO. It's him!"

"Him who? Tammie, what are you talking about?" Caroline wondered.

"NO, it's the guy I stood up last night! I'm not here! Tell him I'm not here! I ran for cover in the bow of the boat, leaving the microwave beeping.

He knocked on the door, "Oh, hi!" Caroline happily greeted him. "Yes, Tammie is here! Hold on I'll get her, she'll meet you on the pier!"

Caroline slid the door closed, "Tammie, you shouldn't be like that. You stood the poor guy up and he must really want to date you. You can't *not* go out there now, I've already told him you're here. Don't be afraid, Tammie. It's okay. Just go out there and tell the guy you'll cook fish for him for dinner."

I came out quietly. "I told you to tell him I wasn't here, Caroline. But I forgive you." This whole encounter had left me fleeing to the shelter of protection in the bow of the boat. I was almost in a panic about facing him after deliberately wasting his time yesterday. However, Caroline helped me through it. I hugged my sister for being persistent with me, and appreciated that she knew my little idiosyncrasies. I knew she meant only the best.

Stephen seemed overjoyed to see me. I felt he was even holding back just how happy he really was. But I didn't get it. Why was he so happy to go out with me? I thought there was an ulterior motive to all men but I had to learn on my own to trust again. We talked and laughed on the dock while I cooked dinner on the charcoal hibachi grill. He loved the fish, saying that it was the best he'd ever tasted!

He informed me that the night before he had literally seen Jimmy Buffet downtown in his *own* bar. We laughed and I had wished I could've seen him too! I apologized for standing him up. We ate and then went for a drive.

He soon learned about my past. He kept asking questions, and more questions. I slowly told him everything. He took me to the big beach on the island and under the shine of the full moon we kissed for what seemed like forever. We kissed some more. I saw fireworks. I felt the starlight glitter beneath my skin, and true-blue iridescent light shimmered all around us. We stayed in each other's arms most of the evening. I didn't really want to ever leave what I felt with him. He had said that he was only in town for that week, that he had no choice but to leave for Virginia Beach, and it made me sad.

He carried the key to my heart. He had said "I promise to never let you go." He did everything in his power to soothe my soul. I overcame so many mountains from that beautifully earnest love that bonded us together as one. He kept traveling back to Key West to see me. It was like nothing I had ever felt before. It was a trust that was deeper than the infinite sky. I was tearing down the walls that had kept me from love.

Love finally had meaning for me with the start at a new kind of life.
A life with a present.
A life with a future.
A life with happiness.
A life with true love.

It was not what I was looking for. It wasn't a chance meeting. We were predestined to meet. That purest of love formed between two tender-hearted individuals that made all the pain from my past melt away with a single kiss–his loving kiss. It all began under the light of the full moon on that Key West night so many years ago!

In the years that followed, I would learn how to love and learn that the world was willing to love me too.

In time, I learned to extend forgiveness to all who had abused me, which gained them the abilities to find that same freedom, if that's what they chose to do. I found forgiveness for myself for the weight I'd always assumed was mine to carry. I informed that wounded little girl inside of me that it was *never* her fault. I loved on her and laid her to rest, deep inside my childhood where she found worthiness and a place where she had always belonged.

This is my story. There *is* life after oppression.

Being different was always my struggle.

Now I am just me.

As I live my life –

Finally Freed!

ABOUT THE AUTHOR

TJ Kechula is a new author who lives in Virginia. She graduated from college in 1996 with a degree in Nursing. She currently lives in Virginia Beach with her husband Mark, who is a 30-year Navy veteran and now a Disney Vacation Planner and founder of Disney Cruising Facebook Group. Her son Tyler also resides in Virginia Beach. He currently attends college with an emphasis on business. Tammie is the daughter of her loving mother, and she has three brothers and sisters along with 36 nieces and nephews. Before she became a fulltime author, she worked with the Hampton Roads flex-pool team in case management which covered seven area hospitals.

It took Tammie 24 years to finally begin writing the story about her journey of survival. It took her almost five years to write, edit, and publish her book.

She enjoys nature, family, and vacationing on Disney Cruises.

Tammie lost her eldest brother Sam to cancer on Thanksgiving Day 2016. She will always remember his earliest interpretation of having been given a terminal diagnosis. He said, "As long as I have a good mind and can rationalize with my body, I can overcome just about anything."

Her favorite bible scripture is Jeremiah 29:11. It reads, "For I know the plans I have for you," declares the LORD, "plans to prosper you and not to harm you, plans to give you hope and a future."

Her own quote reads, "Believe that the injury of your past is not who you are today. It is a symbol of what you overcame. That makes you a survivor and no longer a victim!"

CPSIA information can be obtained
at www.ICGtesting.com
Printed in the USA
FFOW02n0219110718
47395148-50533FF